Humanity at Stake

HUMANITY AT STAKE

On why the world should now end China's
military & political aggression, understand
Taiwan's democracy, and defend 23 million citizens'
human right to self-determination

ABRAHAM YOUNG

All rights reserved. Published in the United States by CreateSpace (http://www.createspace.com) and distributed by Amazon (http://www.amazon.com).

Author's thanks: Another book full with acknowledgments would not suffice all the outpouring of help from so many, but here in particular, the author would like to thank the immense unconditional support of his mother, father, and family; Katherine Chiu (editorial, front cover design, and the world); Alex Young, Marilyn Fu (editorial); Debra Yoo (interior design); HoChie Tsai, Iris Ho, Amy Lin, June Teufel Dreyer, Anthony Kang, Zoe Tseng, Peter Chai, Elizabeth Flynn, Tim Huang, Nick Ramsey, Holiday Dmitri, Kaymaria Daskarolis, Anca Szilagyi, Eric Zamore, Chris Yee, and the countless people who have been so generous in their encouragement, energies, and enthusiasm.

Typeset in Gentium—a typeface for the nations
(http://scripts.sil.org/gentium)

ISBN: 978-1438214115

www.HumanityAtStake.com

For the Taiwanese for their openness and (with hope) their clarity of purpose;

for the Chinese for their openness and (with hope) their willingness to truly engage in peace;

for the Americans for being the source of democratic values & freedoms and (with hope) for their ability to discern among the complicated issue of war, to see in which cases America should stand up to defend, and thereby truly stand with and embody America's great foundational principles;

and for Wang, Chris, and Housing Works, which does immeasurable work for those living with HIV/AIDS, and in their own way, generously picks up the tab for another avenue of neglected human rights in our world.

Interior view of Housing Works Bookstore Café
Website: www.housingworks.org/usedbookcafe

Table of Contents

PART 1: Breaking Silence for the Sake of Understanding

PART 2: Stepping Forward for the Sake of Humanity

Prefatory Note:

The following Parts 1 & 2 depict the true conversation that occurred amongst three inquisitive people who engaged one another.

This document does not purport to present all viewpoints and all narratives on the subject at hand, but instead, seeks to work as an instigator, a starting point, for readers, and readers' own subsequent discussions, and all the conversations, on all levels, that we could all benefit from.

Part 1

Breaking Silence for the
Sake of Understanding

i.   Chance meeting at Housing Works Bookstore Café; basement

I am an American, and I am a Taiwanese-American. I live in New York City.

I volunteer at a not-for-profit bookstore. So does an ethnically Chinese immigrant college student named Wang who grew up the past decade in Japan, and a young American Airlines pilot named Chris who flew aircrafts over the Middle East during the First Gulf War. The bookstore, located on a charming hidden alley right off of the two busiest streets in Manhattan—Houston Street and Broadway—is staffed largely by volunteers like us, and all proceeds go to provide housing for those living with HIV/AIDS in New York. So as would be expected, friendliness is always in abundance, greetings and conversations as we go about our volunteer tasks often veer off into pleasant detours and gregariously long extensions, as none of us are "on the clock," despite being on the job.

So was the case today when Wang (whom I had chatted with in the past about his aspirations to become a journalist), Chris (whom I had just met), and I stood along three sides of a large table in the basement of Housing Works Bookstore Café, stuffing one by one the gigantic mountain of books that stood at the center amongst us, into envelopes for mailing to Internet orders from all across our country and our world.

Nothing dramatic was to happen to any of us by the end of our conversation, and the end of our mountainous task, but an interesting thing would come out of the brief intermingling of our preconceived notions and thoughts, for those few hours exchanged, splayed and mixed across the table. And that interesting thing is a single stripped-down belief, namely the subtitle of this document you hold, "On why the world should now end China's military & political aggression, understand Taiwan's democracy, and defend 23 million citizens' human right to self-determination." After we sealed the last of the fulfilled envelopes, I went upstairs and got caught into reading poetry, the chance to say goodbye to Wang and to Chris passing me by. But anyway I will see them again next week.

It was only after I walked across Broadway, across Houston Street, and eventually back home, that I thought I would write down all that precedes, and all that follows.

ii. Moral dilemma of an American in war

Chris has an atypical schedule. As an aviation pilot, he works only three days of the week, flying round-trip usually, and he has been happy to "do something useful during my downtime in the city," he says as he tapes packing tape on a large envelope and lets out a friendly laugh. He mostly flies to the Caribbean, and his past seventeen years as a commercial pilot in the cockpit, where comfort—for passengers and for himself—is top consideration, have been quite the change from his younger days in the Air Force. We talk a little of our backgrounds, and various cities we have come to love, like beautiful Chicago and sunny Miami and the currently frigid, though still always exciting, New York, and I[1] eventually learn that he came to be a pilot by way of his childhood in the

---

1   Note: I now write this Footnote #1, and all subsequent footnotes, only after all of my memories of that day's conversation—all that you read in the non-footnote body of these pages—had been written down. You will subsequently see many more footnotes appended throughout this document, but please keep in mind: all footnotes are meant as supplemental information for the reader, and unless otherwise specified, they were not a part of the conversation which occurred that day, in the basement of Housing Works Used Books & Café.

Explorer Scouts of Southern California, the vocational arm of Boy Scouts, which led him to eventually serve our country, as they say. When I ask him if he was ever placed into combat situations throughout his experience, he says that although he was personally against anything nuclear, he was at a time tasked for carrying nuclear weaponry on his B-52 Bomber aircraft. Of course, the U.S. never executed anything nuclear during his term of duty at the end of the Cold War into the First Gulf War—those would have been carried only as deterrent. Without wanting to pry, I inarticulately remark something along the lines that it must have been tough to prepare for a mission he was morally against. He either doesn't hear me, or chooses not to, and we end up on the topic of the current Iraq war. He reflects sincerely on the situation, and thinks out loud: "I really feel for those Iraqi kids there now."

He says that nowadays, there are fewer pilots in the military in the role that he was. Technology has fortunately, in ways, exchanged risking human pilots and fliers into battle with sending drones and mechanized force. But unfortunately, in other ways, that has led to an incipient gap, for some, in the bedrock logic to use force only as an absolute, absolute, absolute last resort. "I believe in the need for war in some times," he says, "but somewhere, someone has lost sight of that crucial..." And here, he takes a moment to search for that exact, precise descriptor that culminates his thought: "that crucial *preciousness* of war." I wholeheartedly agree with him, and so do, I think, the millions or even billion people across the world who think (and regret) that America had gone into Hussein's Iraq prematurely, maybe unnecessarily; and similar sentiment goes for all of the other human catastrophes that have happened—a simple proper noun (i.e. Iraq; Vietnam) followed by the word, War—that might have been prevented if the truly precious logic of war, the precious logical mayhem of war, or the lack of either, really, had been fully elicited in *preciousness*, of which human lives are the source and center, and are simply, it.

I take a sip of my still-hot herbal tea, since it is indeed colder here within the exposed stone walls of the employees-only basement, as compared to the upstairs ground floor, wooden, where customers browse, walk around, and relax. I take a moment to stretch my arms (not my legs, because we have been standing this whole time), and I see Wang come down the stairs, dispatched here to help on our mountain of books at center table.

I smile at him and say How's it been going Wang, I missed last week because I was down in Miami for the weekend, and I ask him how his journalism aspirations have been coming along. "It's a lot of work," he says.

"That's what you said the last time—no, the last *few* times I asked you. It must be lots *and lots* of work!" I laugh.

"Yeah, it's always a lot of work. It never ends," he says.

"Yeah, I guess like this pile of books we have here, it never ends; glad you're down here to help, Wang!"

Chris and Wang introduce themselves to one another.

iii. China as many things to as many people

We pack in silence, and once in a while crack a smile, laugh, and point out a title of some book some person somewhere across the world is somehow buying, like "Yoga Booty Ballet Complete Workout Routine" guidebook and DVD. Then we start to chat again.

Chris gets to talking about Shanghai, and how it's really just such an incredible city, and Wang agrees. He says he was born in China; Chris mis-hears and asks, "You said you have never been to China?" Wang says, "No, I said, I *was born* in China," and Chris says Oh, okay, and they go on talking about the dramatic transformations which have taken place in that city, and Chris rhetorically asking, "You haven't been back there for *that many years*? Well you'll be shocked it's changed quite a lot, *quite* a lot," and Wang saying, smiling, "Yes, I know."

I ask Wang something he had mentioned earlier, because I had not been focusing too much on the conversation while taping shut the last few packages: "Wang, you said you were in China until what age? What age did you say?"

Wang says, "Until I was nine. Then I moved to Japan until I came here."

"Ohhhh, cool. So I guess at age nine you still remember being in China then." I am about to add that I lived in Taiwan when I was a kid, from when I was six years old to nine, and I'm glad that I remember having lived there then—in the country that my parents grew up—just like his parallel experience. But something holds me back from voicing my addendum.

Chris mentions, "You know, I was in Beijing once, and I had some leisure time so what I really *really* wanted to do was to go to the National Museum of China, and see this great palace where they have all the national treasures—art, artifacts—from thousands of years of Chinese history." Chris was indeed really in awe, even so recounting it now. However, the story didn't feel likely to have a happy ending. He goes on, "But when I got to Tiananmen Square, went across, to the side where I was told the National Museum was, I couldn't even approach that entire side because they had put up a massive wall, a series of them, and you could see nothing behind it!"

After a pause in reminiscence, Chris continues, "You know, it seems they were digging and digging, and I have no idea what they could have been doing 'cause what do you do with thousands and thousands of years' worth of objects in Chinese history—do you just give all of those historical objects one by one to each family and say, 'Hold on to these for awhile, 'till we're done'?"

Wang affably chuckles at Chris's excitement and humor, and Wang affirms, "Yes, they've been digging for awhile."

I ask when it was that Chris had taken this trip to Beijing, and he answers, a year and a half ago. He adds, "Yeah, so I looked all over the place for clues but all I found were these two girls, students who spoke English, and they just said, 'They'll be digging for the next two years.'"

I haven't been fully paying attention once again, and without taking into account that Chris had this conversation 1.5 years ago, I say in wonderment, "Hmmm, well what're they doing then because the construction won't make it by the Olympics." (In fact, the timing of the Beijing Olympics, which will occur summer of 2008, gives this great construction project on the eastern side of Tiananmen Square enough time to be completed, according to what the two girls had told Chris 1.5 years ago.)

On pace with all their talk about Beijing and Shanghai, I almost decide to interject for no particular reason that I have never been to China my entire life, except briefly to Hong Kong—British Hong Kong—once, before Hong Kong was handed over. But for some reason I decide against mentioning it.

iv. Step right up!:
The kid from Taiwan; the kid from China; and the representative American voice

I finish filling a crate with packaged books, so I carry the filled crate past the rows of shelves located on the other side of the room to the staffers who process the shipping; I come back to our gigantic table with two more empty crates to begin filling. The mountain has subsided, but seems daunting enough to confuse one into thinking: is the mountain somehow growing?

A few books in, when I ask Wang what exactly he's been working on in school, he tells us he wants to write a story about surveillance and the loss of the right to privacy. There begins talk amongst us about the U.S. Patriot Act, then London and *Did you know there're 3 million cameras on their streets!, There're not even enough people to watch all those cameras can you imagine 3 million citizens who are employees paid to watch each one?*, and the reality of solution in place that *Computer programs are written to detect, in aggregate, abnormal activities "seen" on the cameras*, and —*Although I don't even know how it would figure out what "abnormal" means or when it occurs*, Chris says with a disheartened chuckle.

I mention, *Yeah, and you know in China all those monitored bloggers and websites and people, censored and detected by government and being shut down and thrown in jail.*

Wang doesn't deny but points out, *Though there're too many for China's government to keep track; they are losing their power and people are just doing what they want. The Communists are letting down their power. They're really losing their power.*

Chris finds this perspective interesting. "It's interesting you know, me coming from an American's perspective you really just think, you know, *China*—all this intolerance and violating human rights and censorship and centralization. When really, from their perspective, it's probably like what you're saying, Wang: decentralizing, decentralizing, and a relinquishing of their hold over their people over time."[2]

---

2   The conversation of which is the basis for this pamphlet-book took place on February 15th, 2008. General American public opinion and education on the subject of centralized Chinese repression would make a sharp rise a few weeks later, beginning on March 10th after Chinese authorities cracked down with force on Tibetan monk protests, leading to Tibetan uprisings and dozens of deaths and injuries. One focus of international news was China's immediate information blackout following the eruption of violence, and the Chinese government's centralized media control.

According to a *USA Today* news article on March 22nd, 2008:

"Information barely trickled out of the Tibetan capital Lhasa and other far-flung Tibetan communities, where foreign media were banned and thousands of troops dispatched...The Chinese government was attempting to fill the vacuum with its own message. It disseminated footage of Tibetan protesters attacking Chinese and accusations of biased reporting by Western media via TV, the Internet, e-mail and YouTube, which is blocked in China. The communist government's leading newspaper called to 'resolutely crush' the Tibetan demonstrations...

'They've successfully managed the messages available to the average Chinese citizen, and this has fueled broad public support for a heavy-handed approach to controlling unrest,' said David Bandurski, a Hong Kong University expert on Chinese media. 'There will be no nuances to Tibet coverage.'...

At this, inside, and possibly (I could not veil my reaction) outside as well, I shudder, as if a diseased rat, on faulty basis and logic, had been allowed in as a benign fact.

I try to quickly compile my triggered pieces of thought about the increased modes of day-to-day thought-control amongst Chinese citizens that the Chinese Communist Party (CCP) has built up and established throughout the past decade, and the dangers of a single-party government, yes, losing its traditional hold over an accelerating large country, but, as a result, amping up its country's nationalistic fervor and clamping down even more frantically on internal dissent. But all I end up verbalizing is: "Well, the Chinese Communist Party is not going to give up. They're clamping down."

In Chengdu, a sprawling Chinese city at the foot of western China's Tibetan highlands, members of the large Tibetan community complained they could not get telephone calls through to the upland town of Aba where police shot at demonstrators last Sunday...

A group of 29 well-known Chinese dissident writers, lawyers, political activists and other intellectuals decried China's approach to the unrest.

'At present the one-sided propaganda of the official Chinese media is having the effect of stirring up inter-ethnic animosity and aggravating an already tense situation,' said a letter signed by the 29 and circulating via e-mail.

Their appeal, however, was likely to go unheeded by a government that has blacklisted many of the signers for their activism.

The ruling Communist Party's flagship newspaper struck an uncompromising line.

'We must see through the secessionist forces' evil intentions, uphold the banner of maintaining social stability ... and resolutely crush the "Tibet independence" forces' conspiracy,' People's Daily said in an editorial.' (http://www.usatoday. com/news/world/2008-03-22-tibet_N.htm)

Also on that same day, a *UK Times* Online article reported that China has *"imposed a news blackout, authorising only the state Xinhua news agency, China Central Television and Phoenix television to operate in Lhasa, the capital of Tibet...State-run Tibet Television continued to show footage of last week's riots, including scenes of maroon-robed monks throwing rocks at police, protesters kicking in shop fronts and plumes of black smoke from burnt cars. Newsreaders echoed the central government's insistence that the violence was orchestrated by the 'Dalai clique'."* (http://www.timesonline.co.uk/tol/news/ world/asia/article3599803.ece)

—a loud, brief silence spills...

A minor, undefined rift seems to be forming here among us with the mountain of books in between; but Wang, and even more so, Chris, seem not the type to avoid a sensitive topic nor to carry through the conversation with anything but poise, and gregariousness. So...

We go on, albeit with a subtler point of entry.

I say to Chris, "Chris, so have you ever made it to visit Taiwan?"

Chris, without skipping a beat nor showing a crack in his façade to play the conversation along—or so I think—answers No; and then he asks me, "Why?—have you ever been to Taiwan?"

(1) I began this document with this: *I am an American, and I am a Taiwanese-American.* (2) The specifics are these: I had lived in Taiwan for three years when I was a kid, my parents were born and raised in Taiwan, and I have a bunch of relatives there whom I am close with and visit every so often. However, to Chris and Wang, out of the previous two sentences I only mention the latter.

While the atmosphere is pleasant and congenial (by the end, the atmosphere never got unpleasant or uncongenial for any of us, I believe), the initial truths are out.

All our superficial base cards are slapped down in subtext and shown here on the table:

Here's the kid from Taiwan, here's the kid from China, and on the third side of this square table there's the Mr.-All-American pilot, who is intelligent, friendly, has real knowledge of the world, has visited and pondered the cities of China, and though never visited Taiwan, has engaged in U.S. military to deal with the important dilemmas of international relations, overseas.

We have everything we need here for a real simulation—a so-called Strait-talk[3]—with the exclusion of military arms to play offense, defense, and deterrent.

Perfect.

Now: To engage (sans sticks, sans stones), or not to engage?

To proceed and engage: That (I believe) is the answer.

---

3   In 2005, a small group of students at Brown University founded the "Strait-Talk Symposium," bringing together leaders and scholars of various perspectives on the Taiwan-China issue. Most importantly, included was a group of university student delegates from Taiwan, from China, and from America, that concurrently engaged in Interactive Conflict Resolution workshops throughout the week's activities. "The Strait Talk Symposium is an innovative program dedicated to the promotion of open, informed, and creative dialogue on the Taiwan Strait issue... Our goal is increased understanding, especially among the next generation of leaders." —www.straittalk.org

v.   Engagement #1: My opinion, your opinion, my national media, your national media, and the origins of modern-day Taiwan

A dance begins, the steps are on the perimeters of central notions and questions at stake. A contextual echo chamber is softer to bounce off sentiments, for us strangers, currently neighbors at the table.

And so Wang begins with a pointed reminiscence: "I was talking with two friends the other day. It was really, really interesting, because the three of us, were one Taiwanese, me a Chinese, and the other friend from Macao[4]."

"Oh, wow, cool," I remark. I am not sarcastic, I mean it.

"Yeah, it was reaaally interesting because my friend, the Taiwanese, said that she had visited China, and she was surprised how all the things in China that she had heard in Taiwan, weren't there." Wang reiterates the point, "All that she had learned from Taiwan's news wasn't true."

---

4   Macao, like Hong Kong, is a Special Administrative Region of China. After centuries of colonial rule of the Portuguese, Macao was handed over to China in 1999 under the framework of "One Country, Two Systems". In theory, this framework guarantees the autonomy of Macao's legal and economic systems, while Beijing would gain control of the territory's defense and foreign affairs.

I imagine to myself that Wang is referring to, in his Taiwanese friend's experience, her preconception that China is a place of overt suppression—China's human rights abuses having been "smeared" all over Taiwan and the world's media. She probably found no Chinese national suppression while she was a visitor during her PRC stay.

Or maybe, I imagine, growing up in Taiwan, she had an idea that all "Chinese Mainlander Peoples" must be belligerent, disrespectful, and downright disgusting. Probably when she got to China, she did not actually find those Chinese character traits to be in fact true.

But Wang, so far, does not go on to elaborate on which presumptions his Taiwanese friend found to be yarns, upon truly visiting China and meeting the Chinese.

Wang proceeds to say, "Well it surprised me. It was interesting to hear that Taiwan's media controlled by the Taiwanese people make these lies about the Chinese, and everyone always instead insult the Chinese media for being controlled."

I can barely contain all my reactions and rebuttals together to produce a cohesive simple thought—"You know," Wang adds, "in China they show the Taiwan channels on TV, but in Taiwan, they don't allow the China channels on their TV."

Where is he getting these facts from? I highly doubt China would ever allow Taiwan's channels to be broadcast to their public, except maybe soap operas or else just content that was highly filtered under CCP[5] control.

---

5   The CCP is abbreviation for the Chinese Communist Party. By constitution, the CCP is the single ruling party in China's single-party system.

And I don't know if Taiwan broadcasts China's channels in Tai-wan, but, given that China's main channels, the China Central Television, are government-run and its news dictated by the unabashedly official Propaganda Department *of the CCP, why would Taiwan want to?*

Thoughts race through my mind in all directions, but I manage to retort, "Wait a sec. You think somehow the Taiwanese media's controlled? And you somehow think the Chinese media's not??"

At this, Chris, who's been silently observant of late, develops a keen interest and quietly sets down his book for full attention.

I backtrack to elaborate, "Well, hold on, I guess for one thing, the Taiwanese media—you are right in a sense—has been indeed controlled, no, *influenced* more so by a certain political ideology, and that ideology is of the KMT, the Kuomintang,[6] that fled over to Taiwan from China in the late 40's and imposed absolute control over Taiwan's society for the next forty years. For instance, the media when I lived in Taiwan in the early 90's had only three channels on TV, and all three channels were still government-controlled by the KMT."

I am about to make my essential point to Wang—that the modern Taiwanese media, despite its biases over political squab-bles (like America's Fox News vs. CNN),[7] is no longer government-

---

6   The Kuomintang Party ruled China for the decades before the Chinese Civil War, which began in 1945 immediately after WWII. By the end of the Chinese Civil War, the KMT proved unsuccessful against the Communists' uprising, and by 1949 the members and soldiers of the KMT—roughly 2 million people—retreated to the island of Taiwan. In today's democracy on Taiwan, the KMT has become one of the political parties amongst a multi-party system.

7   While the partisan biases in American media sometimes fall one way or other depending on the outlet—FOX News as tending conservative; CCN, liberal—by law, America's media is barred from being owned or controlled by any political party.

controlled in any form, in the way that the Communist-controlled media in China is—but Chris, silent until now, interjects a question. He's a bit confused regarding the status of Taiwan's multiple historical governments, and parties, and acronyms, and that of China's.

(And here, a side note: I myself, upon learning this nuanced collection of Taiwanese historical narrative throughout my college years, have had to help repeat the history and dates to numerous other Taiwanese and non-Taiwanese to start off many conversations about Taiwan and China. And I don't anticipate that necessity to ever cease in my lifetime, nor in the lifetimes of my great-grandchildren, for that matter.

In 1994 Taiwan, the KMT government's monopoly over Taiwan's electronic media became an international affair when KMT authorities conducted "a series of raids on opposition pirate radio stations by seizing their broadcasting equipment in order to cripple their operations." Taiwanese radio host Mr. Hsu Jung-chi staged a hunger strike in Washington D.C., and U.S. Congresspersons held hearings over Taiwan's KMT media monopoly; amongst the comments made, an American journalist testified, "Until the time that independent television and radio stations operate in Taiwan, real democracy will not flourish because governmental accountability will be lacking and real debate during election cycles will not be possible."

In 1995, under intense criticism of their 3-television-station monopoly, the governing KMT party allowed entry of an independent, fourth television station. ("The KMT Retreats on Media Censorship"; *Taiwan Communiqué*, No. 65, April 2005; http://www.taiwandc.org/twcom/65-no4.htm)

In 2005, Taiwan passed a bill to change the national media law enforcement from the Government Information Office—KMT's original censorship and propaganda department during martial law—to a new, non-partisan, independent commission; also, in 2006, due to "general consensus that the media should operate independently and be regulated by a nonpartisan body," the KMT sold its controlling stakes in radio, television, and motion pictures, to private enterprise. ("Media—the Remix"; *Taiwan Review*, Vol.58 No.3 Mar. 2008; http://taiwanreview. nat.gov.tw/ct.asp?xItem=1219&CtNode=128)

However, here, I provide to Chris—though I presume Wang would need the briefing less-so—the abridged summary of what's led to modern-day Taiwan:)

"Chris, so before Taiwan became a fully democratic country the past fifteen years,[8] Taiwan was ruled by the KMT, or the Kuomintang Nationalist Party, since the late-40's."

Chris nods at this. I'm glad to see that Chris already seems more knowledgeable than average. I go on, "The origins of the KMT began on China when the Republic of China was formed under Sun Yat-sen after the collapse of the last dynasty, the Qing Dynasty, in 1911. The Republic of China subsequently was the government of China until the Communists successfully rose up against the KMT in the years after 1945,[9] and the leaders of the KMT and their army fled from China to the island of Taiwan, with the continuation of their Republic of China, on Taiwan."

Chris then asks, "So, the KMT, in their minds, had come to Taiwan just temporarily?" Chris is visibly intrigued.

I feel the joy of an educator in the presence of a keen, inquisitive student, and I answer, "Yeah, the KMT had fled across the Strait to Taiwan with just the plan to set up temporary base, and eventually regroup to 'take back China' from the Commu-

---

8   My mention to Chris of 15 years of democracy in Taiwan, as of 2008, is an approximation. The exact number of years since Taiwan's full democracy is closer to 12 years, because in 1996 Taiwan had its first genuine, multi-party Presidential elections. Before 1996, those so-called "elections" that took place in Taiwan only featured 1-party on the ballot, and that party was the ruling KMT. The 1996 elections culminated nearly a decade of gradual reforms and opening up for freedom of speech and freedom of press since the 1987 lifting of martial law on the island.

9   The year 1945, significantly, was the year of defeat for the Japanese at the end of WWII. When the Japanese army, once the common enemy of the KMT and the Chinese Communists, ceased to unite the KMT-Communist alliance, the power struggle between these two groups soon escalated into full-scale civil war.

nists. From the time they landed on Taiwan and for the next 20, 30 years, that was their main and ultimate goal."

I have come to an essential, a major wall that requires consideration in the structure of a cross-strait debate or discussion.

"But one important thing to note," I say, "in understanding the current events is that the KMT *does not equal* to Taiwan. That's a common cause of confusion about modern-day Taiwan. But in fact, not only if you consider the democratic pluralism, if you look at the origins of people on Taiwan, the ratio, those that came over with the KMT government/army only comprise under 15% of the people in Taiwan, whereas the other 85% of people came to Taiwan since the 15th and 16th centuries, have lived in Taiwan for fifteen generations or else were original aborigines on the island before the KMT came."

I add, "Even more so, when the KMT fled to Taiwan they enacted absolute suppression of the Taiwanese people. There were massacres of tens of thousands of Taiwanese people starting in 1947 by the KMT, government-conducted political imprisonments, vanishings, and assassinations, and for the next decades,[10]

---

10   The "White Terror" period of martial law in Taiwan—which began on February 28th, 1947, in the so-called "2-28 Massacre"—lasted for forty years until the lifting of martial law on July 15th, 1987.

An article in the *New York Times* on March 28th, 1947, reported:

"Foreigners who have just returned to China from Formosa corroborate reports of wholesale slaughter by Chinese troops and police during anti-Government demonstrations a month ago.

These witnesses estimate that 10,000 Formosans were killed by the Chinese armed forces...

The anti-Government demonstrations were said to have been by unarmed persons whose intentions were peaceful...

Foreigners who left Formosa a few days ago say that an uneasy peace had been established almost everywhere, but executions and arrests continued...

An American who had just arrived in China from Taihoku said that troops from the mainland arrived there March 7 and indulged in three days of indiscriminate killing and looting. For a time everyone seen on the streets was shot at, homes were broken into and occupants killed. In the poorer sections the streets were said to have been littered with dead.

There were instances of beheadings and mutilation of bodies, and women were raped, the American said...

The people were machine gunned. Groups were rounded up and executed. The man who had served as the town's spokesman was killed. His body was left for a day in a park and no one was permitted to remove it.

A Briton described similar events at Takao, where unarmed Formosans had taken over the running of the city. He said that after several days Chinese soldiers from an outlying fort deployed through the streets, killing hundreds with machine-guns and rifles and raping and looting. Formosan leaders were executed. Thousands were thrown into prison, many bound with thin wire that cut deep into the flesh.

The foreign witnesses reported that leaflets signed with the name of Generalissimo Chiang Kai-shek, promising leniency, and urging all who had fled to return, were dropped from airplanes. As a result many came back to be imprisoned or executed. 'There seemed to be a policy of killing off all the best people,' one foreigner asserted.

The foreigners' stories are fully supported by reports of every important foreign embassy or legation in Nanking..."

An article appearing in *The Nation* on May 24th, 1947, reported the events that led up to the massacres:

"On February 27 a policeman of the Taiwan (Formosa) Monopoly Bureau saw a woman selling smuggled cigarettes on the streets of the capital, Taipeh. When he tried to seize her tray and money, she pulled away, and he struck her a crashing blow on the head with his revolver butt. She died at his feet. An angry mob gathered, and the police shot into the crowd, killing one person and wounding others. Forthwith a year and a half of gathering hatred for an inefficient, autocratic, corrupt administration exploded into unarmed demonstrations against the mainland Chinese.

China put down the revolt with brutal repression, terror, and massacre. Mainland soldiers and police fired first killing thousands indiscriminately; then, more selectively, hunted down and jailed or slaughtered students, intellectuals, prominent business men, and civic leaders..." (New York Times & The Nation digital arcives; http://www.taiwandc.org/hst-1947.htm)

A *Taiwan Journal* article in 2007 announced findings of "a special report conducted by the Government Information Office...[that] in the first five years of the 1950s, the ruling KMT-led regime on Taiwan executed at least 4,000 to 5,000 people it branded as Chinese Communist spies. These included intellectuals, culturati, workers and farmers. It sentenced a similar number of people to prison with sentences of between 10 years and life .... official records from the Ministry of Justice ... indicated around 140,000 people were court-martialed in 29,407 cases..." (http://taiwanjournal.nat.gov.tw/ct.asp?CtNode=122&xItem=24431). Moreover,

Taiwanese were not allowed to speak up, or even speak their own Taiwanese language—were forced to speak Chinese."

At this last series of fact, Chris expresses a genuine knowledge spark, a quenched curiosity: "What? Really?"—rhetorical exclamations, once again. "You know, as Americans we've always been taught that the KMT…"

He need not finish his sentence, because I have already heard the mistaken notion before—one other common cause of confusion over Taiwan.

I can't resist picking up his thread: "—Yeah," I say, "in the decades after the Communists took over China, the democratic world saw the KMT as the benevolent hedge against Communism in China, against Communism in Asia. But being anti-Communist—the KMT—did not equate to being pro-democracy in their rule over Taiwan. Much the opposite.

"But that common misperception about the KMT is understandable, if you consider that during that time America was embroiled with anti-Communism sentiment, so it was hard to view the KMT as anything but good."

"Wow," says Chris, truly excited. "It is really so interesting, coming from my own perspective, and having had, having heard

---

along with this ban on government opposition during martial law, Taiwanese were restricted from speaking about the traumatic massacres that took place. This ingrained taboo has lasted until the opening up of speech and dialogue in the recent years, such as the creation of the 2-28 Memorial Park in Taipei; movies on the subject such as Hou Hsiao-Hsien's internationally acclaimed *A City of Sadness*; or the upcoming U.S. film, *Formosa Betrayed*, exploring how the KMT's spy network extended into the United States, leading to the assassination of a Carnegie-Melon University Taiwanese professor in 1981; the historic "2-28 Hand-in-Hand" rally in Taiwan in 2004, when 2-million Taiwanese formed a 500-km human chain from the southern tip to the northern tip of the island; and the designation of February 28th as Taiwan's "National Peace Memorial Day".

others talk about China, the KMT and the 'Province of Taiwan'; and now you're telling me all this about Taiwan!"

It gives me a happy rush of endorphins to inform someone of what I know about how this came to be, this modern-day Taiwan. And here I was getting through past the clichés, into the nuances, discussing with an enthusiastic Chris, and a pilot at that!

I ride the wave to present day chronology: "And so eventually, Taiwan evolved to become fully democratic, and actually, in 2000 another party was voted into office. The election and transition of power were all carried through and done peacefully; the KMT was voted out, out for the first time ever since they fled China and set up government on Taiwan. The KMT have now been out of office for the past eight years. A real democratic transition of power."[11] I am proud as I describe this to Chris, despite that I wonder whether, to Wang, this might sound like some sort of gloating.

Upon realizing that I almost forgot to include the international context in all of this, I continue, "But of course, somewhere in the 70's and 80's, post-Cold War, the U.S. and other major coun-

---

11   Only five weeks after our conversation took place, on March 22nd, 2008, Taiwan held its fourth presidential elections. The Democratic Progressive Party, which had been in control of Taiwan's executive branch the past two terms from 2000-2008, was voted out in favor of the Kuomintang party. This marked Taiwan's second peaceful transition of power to an opposition political party through the democratic process. In regard to Taiwan's maturing democracy, this successful electoral event was noted by the international community in statements such as that of Canada's Minister of Foreign Affairs ("The smooth and orderly elections came after a vigorous campaign, demonstrating that democracy is laying down strong roots."—statement released on international.gc.ca) and Britain's Foreign Minster ("The successful Presidential elections in Taiwan today are testament to Taiwan's democracy."—statement released on fco.gov.uk).

tries switched their official recognition of China from the KMT, located on Taiwan, to the Communist Party in Beijing."

In all of this, I forget to observe whether Wang is not paying attention because he already knows all the history that I have laid out, or if he's seething at the mouth to combat me (that absolutely was not the case, but O, my uncontrolled imagination!), or if he has ready to tell his own series of historical rebuttals to discount my narrative about the status of Taiwan.

I am hard-pressed to ever hear anyone, though,—whether KMT, DDP, CCP, Taiwanese or Chinese, Icelandic or whatever—discount any of the factual details I have laid out for how the modern-day democracy of Taiwan has come to be; and I would welcome—genuinely welcome, without sarcasm—any further undisputable facts about, or against, Taiwan as the free democracy in Asia that it is. Or better yet, please—someone—do offer the political narrative, which I have allotted no space at all in this document to expound, why modern-day China has felt it its inherent business and right to militarily and politically force Taiwan into submission under China's own definition of a separate country's nationhood, or supposed lack thereof.

Obviously, I have become riled up. But not an ounce, in any sense, to attack, but only, singularly, to truly defend.

Images Relating to Taiwan's 2-28 Massacre

228 Incident (The Terrible Inspection). Woodcut printmaking, ca. 1947. Jun Li (Rong-zan Huang).

This wall poster at Taipei's 2-28 Memorial Museum depicts a massacre by KMT troops of Taiwanese civilians at Keelung Harbour. Incredibly, one man survived and lived to tell the tale.

Taiwanese citizen killed by the KMT Army in the White Terror after the 2-28 Incident.

The 2-28 Monument, unveiled on February 28th, 1997,
located near the Presidential Office in Taipei.

vi. Interim tit-for-tat: What in heaven and in hell is Taiwan—to whom?

We had gotten sidetracked. Wang has another few points to make:

"My Taiwanese friend, she herself also said that the voting in Taiwan is very corrupt. That people give money to vote and that elections are corrupt there anyway."

I consider the facts I've heard about cases of vote-buying in Taiwan, and the strong tendency to vote according to local allegiances in various Taiwanese localities. But then I keep in mind the larger context of our conversation: Taiwan's truly successful functional democracy as a country—even hailed as Asia's "model democracy"[12]—in comparison to China or other non- or semi-democratic countries or regions (e.g. Hong Kong or Nepal).

I respond to Wang, "Yes, I think those corrupt things do occur in Taiwan. And I think Taiwan has a lot of internal issues

12   Since the 1990s, due to Taiwan's unique transition in Asia from authoritarianism towards gradual constitutional freedoms and the establishment of democratic practices, Taiwan has been termed a "model democracy" by top American political leaders, U.S. House and Senate Resolutions, and academic and mainstream papers.

about the motivations behind people's vote, like for instance my grandparents: my grandparents came over with the KMT so they have a very different view of Taiwan and its relation to China, than, say, the view of my dad (their son), who was born and grew up in Taiwan.

"But anyway," I try to be conscious not to get sidetracked, "the real issue is as a whole, along the path Taiwan has traveled over recent decades to our present reality of the past 15 years, whether it is now as a nation a transparent, functional, and free democracy, where people can, and do, choose. And yes, that is the case."

I notice Chris unconsciously nodding his head in agreement. I point out a fact in a metric we can all understand and grasp in America: "And you know, voter participation in the presidential elections since '96 has consistently exceeded 75% of the population, so people are definitely excited to vote; they are excited to have that freedom, finally, and I can't believe that a single person would willingly give up that freedom now."

Strong statistics and figures often stump even the most prolific conjecturer. >75% voter turnout, according to my own American standards (U.S. voter turnout usually moseys around 50%, and in my lifetime peaked only at 55% in 2004), seems impressive; but I am unsure of how indicative that high turnout is of Taiwanese voters' pure excitement to participate in elections, rather than a vote cast out of fear of (or anger at) the imminent threat created by China's missiles. In any case, Wang moves on to the subsequent point, recounted from that interesting conversation with his Taiwanese friend:

"My friend," Wang says, "told me that she likes China more than Taiwan, after she came to visit China. And she's Taiwanese."

Ten seconds ago I had blunted Wang's stab at Taiwan's corrupt electioneering with a democracy statistic. But at once, here, on the other hand, Wang has stumped everything I was thinking about. Simply with mention of his Taiwanese friend who "likes China more." There is no discursive truth I have that could challenge that.

So instead I ask a question: "Did your friend's parents grow up in Taiwan?"

"Yes," Wang replies, "but I think her grandfather fought for the KMT or something."

That piece of information was background that would have been significant from the start, I think to myself. But I don't say to Wang.

vii. Engagement #2: Hawaii = a part of America.
      Taiwan ≠ a part of China.

"I think the Taiwanese, the Taiwan's leadership, I mean, overreact," says Wang.

Overreact?

I imagine that I see, out of the corner of my eye, Chris, in his mind, agreeing with this conjecture *that the Taiwanese and Taiwan's leadership OVERREACT.* I cringe, but don't panic because this has become too commonplace, that Chris has taken at face value the media headlines!, the ingrained clichés!, that

Taiwan leadership = always "provoking China"
= always "provoking" the situation = overreact,

and that which Wang now uses as a talking point. In my mind, I think all the Chinese leverage in America, the Chinese influences, the media spin doctors, or lethargic media regurgitators, have nudged someone like Chris in chorus over time so that at any moment, even *he* could begin treating Taiwan—

Taiwan's hard won democracy, Taiwan's admirable legacy and spirit of freedom in the face of suppression, democracy's subsequent victory, Taiwan's aggregate and tangible yearning, embodied in Taiwan's 23 million people, to voice their finally democratic self-governing nationhood, on the world stage—

all as a simple nuisance, a mouse's provocation, some accepted fact that when the giant cat next door has plugged up all holes and boxed one in unhealthy isolation, one should simply keep quiet, sit tight, and ignore one's own starvation.

Where do I begin to respond? I start to say, "The situation now is like this." And here, I direct my words more towards Chris since it has been more common than not for Americans (the average American, the American media, and even some American politicians) to misunderstand Taiwan's current operational nationhood. Also, for some particular reason, a latched desire to inform the basic, the *de facto* realities about Taiwan to Chris has landed upon me, like a seed that has fallen into my palm that I now must absolutely plant.

I continue, "In all forms of any country's operation—national, international, local, political government, economy, healthcare, military, education, borders, and all the rest—Taiwan is likewise completely functional on its own, and completely separate of China's government. The People's Republic of China does not have a single office, nor a single person, nor a single hand in any of Taiwan's domestic operations, and has never had, not for a single day."

Chris is perplexed. "You serious? Wait, you really mean, never?"

I think to myself the historical narratives of each side... the People's Republic of China (PRC) established in 1949 by the Communists... the Republic of China (ROC) established in 1911 in China, and subsequently, when the PRC elbowed them out, the Kuomintang (KMT) transporting their ROC government to Taiwan... decades later in Taiwan, the eventual remaking of the KMT to abolish its outdated goals to "retake the Mainland," and the reformation of Taiwan's political system...

Chris continues to ask, "So who was in control of Taiwan before the KMT came?"

"The KMT came a few years after Wold War Two, and before World War Two Taiwan was controlled by the Japanese." For a few seconds, I think over my history... "So the Japanese had colonized Taiwan since 1895, before that the colonizers were Chinese, but in the past centuries in all, Taiwan had been under colonization at different points by the Dutch, the Portuguese, the Chinese, and the Japanese. [13]

13
- In 1594, despite aborigines who already inhabited the island, Portuguese explorers "discovered" the land, calling it *Ilha Formosa*—or, "Beautiful Island."
- Throughout the 17th and 18th century, waves of Chinese immigrants traveled across the Taiwan Strait to settle temporarily and permanently in this "haven for antigovernment intellectuals as well as the economically dispossessed."
- The Dutch landed on its coasts in 1624 and for the next four decades, they "undertook the first serious effort at developing Taiwan," in terms of its infrastructure, labor, government, and agriculture.
- In 1662, a large force of troops that "fought against the new Manchu regime in China in support of the outgoing Ming dynasty" were defeated, and in retreat, they turned their focus "on the Dutch presence in Taiwan," successfully driving out the Dutch. For the next twenty years, to the Qing dynasty, Taiwan "still represented a possible staging area for attacks against the mainland."

"So anyways, the Japanese were the government of Taiwan from 1895 to World War Two, and they had successfully built up a lot of Taiwan's infrastructures, there've always been a lot of Japanese influences in Taiwan, like Japanese food, Japanese-style apartments, and some older educated-Taiwanese speak Japanese—but of course, Japan then was still, at times, iron-fisted in their colonization, so things weren't great for Taiwanese."

Again, I have gotten sidetracked—sidetracking often happens in trying to set the foundation for Taiwan.

"In any case," I continue, "the point here is that the PRC has not had any physical presence in Taiwan, but they claim to everyone in the world, with a straight face, that currently, 'Taiwan is a province of China.' Everyone who hasn't bought into China's fantasy knows, obviously, that Taiwan is and has been a completely separate entity than China except in name, so it's the old story of the emperor's clothes."

- In 1683, the Qing decided to send a large force to Taiwan for the purpose of finally expelling the Ming-loyalists. The next two centuries involved "nominal Qing dynasty rule over Taiwan." Several factors and uprisings "made Taiwan difficult for the Chinese central government," and as a result, "The challenge of effectively governing Taiwan was beyond the Qing's ability and commitment."
- In 1895, after China's defeat in the Sino-Japanese War, China ceded Taiwan to Japan.

Regarding Taiwan's growth "within China's shadow," Denny Roy, Senior Research Fellow at the Asia-Pacific Center for Security Studies, writes: "The people who became known as the Taiwanese came to Taiwan to get away from conditions in China. Taiwan became a place where Chinese individuals and communities could make a fresh start. This was the beginning of Taiwan's divergence from the mainland in social, economic, and political development. From here foreign influences would play an important role as well—first the Dutch and then, more profoundly, the Japanese." (Denny Roy, *Taiwan: a Political History* (New York: Cornell University Press, 2003), 13-32)

From Chris's face, I can tell, or so I imagine, that his pre-conception—based on all the confusion and ingrained drilling of words, "Taiwan" "province" "a part of China"—must have assumed that there had to be at least some sort of governmental Chinese arm, however miniscule, currently operating on Taiwan. But that is not so; and he slowly grasps this simple, yet hesitant, fact.

To seal the deal, I refer close to home once again: "The way Hawaii is a state of the US—where Hawaiians pay federal taxes, the federal government faculties extend to Hawaii, and if some disaster occurs in Hawaii, there is inherent physical relationship between state and its nation—Taiwan, on the other hand, has nothing to do with China and Beijing."

As Chris ponders this new knowledge, and I assume Wang prefers not mentioning this old knowledge (or maybe he, too, is ignorant of this), I go on:

"Okay look,—and here's one grave problem amongst many—when SARS broke out in Taiwan and Taiwan and the world was dealing with it, Taiwan was the only one left out of international communications and coordinated emergency management. Why? Because China claimed Taiwan is a province of China. China declared, *Taiwan is a part of China; our province! We will take care of them, this domestic territory.* But of course China had no capability nor intention to do anything (except to make sure that no other countries acknowledged Taiwan's obvious sovereignty, that no country went in to Taiwan to help, without going through China's 'approval' first). Moreover, Taiwan has always been, and still is, excluded from the World Health Organization.[14] Because of all

14   Taiwan has been petitioning every year since 1997 to participate in the World Health Organization, and every year it has failed. As a result, Taiwan's doctors and hospitals are denied access to WHO information, and even Taiwan's journalists are barred from participation in WHO activities.

In 1998, soon after Taiwan's first failed attempt to join the WHO, Taiwan suffered a health emergency when "the WHO was unable to assist Taiwan with an outbreak of enterovirus 71 which killed 70 Taiwanese children and infected more than 1,100 Taiwanese children." (US Senate Resolution 26, "Relating to Taiwan's Participation in the World Health Organization") (http://www.taiwandc.org/nws-9851.htm)

In a 2007 article by Bob Dole, published in the *Washington Times* in the days before that year's annual World Health Assembly meeting, he wrote:

"The case for admitting Taiwan to WHO could not be clearer:

(1) Taiwan has the resources to become a top-tier participant. In the last 10 years, its public and private sectors have provided more than $450 million in health care and humanitarian aid to more than 90 countries. Today, with one of the world's 20 largest economies, it is willing and able to do much more.

(2) Taiwanese doctors and other health-care professionals have the skills to provide services to the widest possible range of beneficiaries. At home, their dedication and implementation of a superior health-care system has led The Economist *to rank Taiwan the second-healthiest nation in the world.*

(3) Taiwan is uniquely placed to address health threats emanating from China and elsewhere in Asia. Having suffered from the SARS epidemic, which began in China in 2003, Taiwan worked closely and directly with other Asian countries in 2005 to prevent the spread of the bird flu (H5N1 influenza). Taiwan's full-fledged campaign made it the only East Asian country to escape this pandemic.

Unfortunately, Taiwan's efforts to increase its health-care outreach and its effectiveness through cooperation with WHO are actively and constantly thwarted by communist China and WHO itself. Beijing, an authoritarian regime, vigorously opposes every attempt by Taiwan, a vibrant democracy, to participate in international organizations...

An example of how this translates into action and inaction is WHO's refusal to allow Taiwan to take part in conferences on the bird flu. In the critical initial stages of the SARS outbreak, WHO and China refused to share information with Taiwan, thereby putting Taiwan and many other countries at greater risk. Recently, WHO signed a secret memorandum with China requiring that WHO obtain China's permission before sharing information with Taiwan or inviting Taiwanese doctors or officials to conferences.

At the same time, WHO has extended membership or observer status to such nonstates as the Cook Islands, the Sovereign Order of Malta, the Vatican and even the Palestine Liberation Organization. Yet Taiwan, which is genuinely positioned to contribute hundreds of millions of dollars and serve as a barrier to the spread of sudden disease outbreaks, remains locked out...

these factors, caused by China's insistence that the world adopt

Admitting Taiwan to WHO is not only in Taiwan's interests and those of other countries that support disease eradication and prevention and improved health care standards; it is also directly in U.S. interests. There are 170,000 Americans resident in Taiwan, and our country provides 22 percent of WHO's budget.

I appeal to President Bush and his representatives to WHO, as well as those of the world's other democracies, to stand up to the WHO's bureaucracy and the regime in Beijing by voting to grant full WHO membership to Taiwan.

The world is a dangerous enough place already. We should not allow political obstructions to tie Taiwan's hands and deny those in need the benefit of its health-care talents and economic largess." (http://worldhealthtaiwan.googlepages. com/2op-edarticlesontaiwan%27swhoinclusion)

Within days of Bob Dole's *Washington Times* article, the President of Taiwan, Chen Shui-bian, also published the following words in the *Washington Post*:

"While disease heeds no national borders, Taiwan has had to fight pandemics without help from the World Health Organization—a humanitarian agency that is supposed to serve all humankind...

The WHO secretariat has effectively jeopardized the health of people in Taiwan and other countries.

For a decade, we have striven relentlessly to participate in the WHO, to no avail. Even our humble pursuit of "meaningful participation" has yielded little success. With 95 percent of the Taiwanese people supporting full WHO membership, I must act upon the will of my people as a democratically elected president. ...

Taiwan, formally known as the Republic of China, is indisputably a sovereign state, satisfying all of the criteria cited in Article 1 of the Montevideo Convention on the Duties and Obligations of States. It has a permanent population, a defined territory, a functional government and the capacity to conduct relations with other states. It also has its own internationally traded currency and issues its own passport, honored by virtually all other nations.

Another broadly affirmed criterion for recognizing the legitimacy of a state is the principle, enunciated in the U.N. Universal Declaration of Human Rights, that the sovereignty a state exercises should be based on the will of the people. A truly "sovereign" state, in other words, is free and democratic. We find no better words to describe Taiwan.

Ultimately, the question of Taiwan's participation in the WHO is a moral one. The systematic shunning of Taiwan is unconscionable not only because it compromises the health of our 23 million people but also because it denies the world the benefit of our abundant public health and technical resources...

As humankind seeks to control global pandemics, victory will require collaboration that is not restricted by political obfuscation or subject to discriminatory picking and choosing of participants. We must not allow an all-but-one scenario to undermine our common mission—health for all." (http://worldhealthtaiwan.googlepages. com/2op-edarticlesontaiwan%27swhoinclusion)

the Chinese view and isolate Taiwan, the Taiwanese doctors, hospitals, health officials, the dying and vulnerable patients, and all the people in the country were really left to fend for themselves during SARS."

viii. Engagement #3: Taiwan's "overreactions"— Why? China's offensive weapons justification—Where?

I have managed to stay cordial, but it is evident that I have brought to the surface issues that I am passionate about. I do not know Chris and Wang too well, so I can't guess their threshold for being turned off by confrontation; but these are truths I must tell, truths that must be told, and heard, for everyone's sake. However, I take a break from speaking, and decide to see what they might have to say.

Wang reiterates, "I think the Taiwanese, the Taiwan's leadership, I mean, overreact." I guess Wang is not convinced. And I guess I had not answered his question—I mean, his comment—directly the first time. But then again, his comment is quite vague.

"How so?" *How does Taiwan's leadership overreact. I guess... I guess some might say they do, even many Taiwanese voters feel that they do.* "I'm just not quite sure what you mean. I mean, it's not like there's just this harmless issue lying around and Taiwan is just making some useless fuss over it—"

"But I think Taiwan always reacts to everything," says Wang. "And China just doesn't usually talk about it, their stance is, Don't fight over it now and it'll go away or resolve itself," and in his eyes and the confident tone he verbalized China's attitude, I see that he agrees with China's *more peaceful approach*, as he puts it.

"—but what I was saying," I pick up again, "is that Taiwan is not making some comments and 'fuss' over status for no reason at all: China has hundreds of ballistic missiles aimed at Taiwan, from right across the Taiwan Strait." I have stressed this fact to so many different people, in countless conversations, that sometimes the fact—that China has these invasion-ready missiles aimed at Taiwan—simply becomes a menacing, yet boring, fact.

But then I imagine, or have dreams, about those missiles, one terrible day, launched *en masse* across the Taiwan Strait onto the tiny island. The nightmarish human catastrophes that would ensue...—I develop all this anxiety—and I imagine how my relatives felt during the '96 China "missiles tests" into Taiwan territorial waters.[15] "Wang, those numbers of missiles have been growing by over a hundred, every single year—look, when I started looking

---

15   After the 1950's territorial military conflicts in the Taiwan Strait between the KMT and Chinese Communists over the Yijiangshan, Matsu, and Kinmen Islands, the next military confrontations occurred four decades later when China conducted "missile tests" during what is termed the "1995-1996 Taiwan Strait Crisis".

To the objections of China, in 1995, the United States granted a visa to Taiwan's President Lee Teng-hui after he was invited to deliver a speech at the Cornell University reunion. A *Time* magazine article that appeared a week before the visit noted: *"Beijing's protests were unusually fierce. Foreign Minister Qian Qichen summoned the U.S. Ambassador, J. Stapleton Roy, for a diplomatic dressing down. As Defense Minister Chi Haotian's scheduled visit this month to the U.S. was postponed, the People's Daily thundered, 'We demand that the American government rescind this wrongful decision.'"* (http://www.time.com/time/magazine/article/0,9171,982997-1,00.html)

At both six and nine weeks after Taiwan President Lee's visit, China's Peoples Liberation Army launched a series of military demonstrations and "missile tests" in close range to Taiwan, prompting the United States to mobilize and station aircraft carriers near the Taiwan Strait. (http://www.globalsecurity.org/military/ops/taiwan_strait.htm)

into all this maybe six years ago, I remember telling people about China's missiles pointed at Taiwan, just like I am telling you now. But back then, there were 600 missiles. And the next year, when I told someone else, by then there were over 700 missiles. Skip ahead just some years, and now, when I try to tell people, I have to refer to the painful number that there are now over 1,200 Chinese missiles pointed right at Taiwan."[16] *Their military is only growing*

In 1996, in the weeks leading up to Taiwan's first democratic presidential elections, China again fired a series of "missile tests" dangerously close to Taiwan's coast. The impetus for China's aggression was not meant to be concealed: "The Chinese acknowledged that the tests are designed to intimidate Taiwan as that country's first direct national presidential election approached." While the U.S., along with other countries, condemned China's actions as "provocative and reckless," China's spokesperson responded, "Actually it is China who should be protesting, because the question of Taiwan is entirely China's internal affair, in which no other country has the right to interfere." (http://www.cnn.com/WORLD/9603/china_taiwan/08/index.html)

China sought to intimidate Taiwan voters from voting for the KMT incumbent candidate, Lee Tung-Hui; but opposite to their intentions, China's military aggression actually prompted Taiwanese voters to vote in favor of Lee, even more so.

16   At the time of our conversation on February 15th, the 2008 Security Report from Taiwan's National Security Council had not been released. On March 26th, that Report gave the newest numbers:

"...tactical ballistic missiles deployed by China against Taiwan reached more than 1,400 at the end of last year...

The council said the deployment 'allows the People's Liberation Army (PLA) to launch a nine-wave, 12-hour saturation missile attack on Taiwan and conduct precision strikes on more than 100 key targets in Taiwan.'...

...The number of its new large-sized naval vessels and submarine-launched anti-ship submarines had increased to 30 each by the end of last year, which, together with the deployment of YJ-62A anti-ship cruise missiles, equipped the [PLA navy] with the capability to blockade the Taiwan Strait, the northeastern and southwestern waters of Taiwan proper,'...

...the PLA Air Force (PLAAF) was preparing to deploy 200km-range S-300 PMU2 anti-aircraft missiles, which, along with its new-generation Air Early Warnings, electric warfares, and more than 10 types of stand-off weapons, 'had reduced Taiwan's strategic depth and imposed threats to military and civil aviation in the airspace around Taoyuan and Hsinchu.'

like wild-fucking-crazy, and the tremendous extent of the PLA's[17] *aggres-*
sive build-up has all been well-documented.

However, this last point does not even need to be made to
Wang and Chris, as their silence, their silence at the painful reality
of 1,200-plus Chinese missiles aimed at Taiwan shows that there is
no single argument—moral, logical, or just—that validates China's
past and present military aggression and missile arsenal, much
less the continued growth on both menacing counts, which has
been clearly the case.

Not just in reference to the basement where Wang, Chris,
and I now stand, the real elephant in the room is this: not a single
person, up through the highest levels of government, within China, the US, or Taiwan is capable of providing a single validating
argument for this.

---

*...the PLAAF had increased its fleet of new-generation fighter aircraft of various types
at a rate of 70 a year, with the number growing to 550 by the end of last year.*

*The Chinese military's successful test-firing in January of its Dong Feng 25 ballistic
missile against a weather-satellite marked significant progress in China's space technology
in terms of satellite tactical communications, satellite electronic reconnaissance, satellite
oceanic navigation and satellite meteorological observation...*

*'The PLA possesses all-day technology for aerial surveillance, satellite imagery and to-
pography, which can enhance its ability to precisely attack targets in Taiwan,"...*

...China had revealed its ambition to expand its sea power to the high seas.

*'In 2007, China's ocean exploration ships conducted 14 sorties in the waters around
Taiwan in the name of oceanic survey, intelligence and technology,'..."* (http://www.tai-
peitimes.com/News/front/archives/2008/04/04/2003408230)

17   The unified military organization of China is called the People's Liberation
Army, or PLA.

Part 2

Stepping Forward for the Sake of Humanity

ix.   A new approach to engagement

So far, I realize, I have been on the defensive. Busy with re-
sponding—and reacting—first, to accusations from Wang about
Taiwan's media supposedly being propagandistic, then about
Taiwan's elections supposedly being a farce "because of the cor-
ruption anyways"; with explaining to Chris that Taiwan has not
been controlled by China/CCP and is currently a *de facto* sovereign democratic nation; and with debating the expected-but-still-
shocking accusation that Taiwan (instead of militaristic China)
has constantly been the one "provoking" and "overreacting." On
the defensive, I have not had a moment to question and interro-
gate Wang on China and the CCP's actions.

For a second I think, *maybe that is China's strategy: to cry
bloody murder at every move of Taiwan, the 'overreacting' 'renegade
province,' so that the international community seldom has a moment to
consider the basic realities in China's aggressive stance, not to mention
Taiwan's present democracy and sovereignty and therefore, the human
right of Taiwanese to be free from China's constant military aggression.*

If that really has been China's strategy, I guess China's strategy has worked thus far, because, consider this:

When is the last time anyone saw any mainstream media coverage about China's build-up of missiles aggressively directed at Taiwan, and the human rights issues involved there?

Who has ever rigorously sought China's explanation (lack thereof) for why they feel the right to intimidate 23 million free people to submit to their imaginary will?

Where's the megaphone?? So far on the world stage, definitely not in the hands of the democratic Taiwanese peoples.

So far in our conversation, our format has been a format of brief supposition/question directed at me, and elongated responses and attempts at answers out of my brain and out of my mouth. I desire to change the format a bit, or at least turn the tables.

"So I've always been curious," I say to Wang, "about people with a Chinese view of Taiwan."

For a moment Wang glances into the distance to consider my new tone, noticing how different the conversation suddenly feels, but does not raise his eyes to meet mine. I continue, "Where do you think people with a Chinese view get their information and develop those views from?, 'cause they almost always seem very sure of what Taiwan's status is, or should be."—namely, of course, that Taiwan is supposedly unified with China, its given 'motherland' of some sort—"So where, for example, do you think you got your thoughts on Taiwan?"

Wang sees, from my question, a weakness in his own accusations. But he is fair enough not to attempt holding back his response: "Mostly from China's media."

I do not probe further on this particular point. To the three of us, I think the point is more than apparent.

I decide to move on to a central pillar in international context: "And I am always curious about the people with a Chinese view of Taiwan: What is the basis for their belief that Taiwan must, or at the least should, be annexed into China (assuming this person doesn't already believe that Taiwan is 'currently a part of China'). So what are the reasons, why do you think Taiwan should annex into China?"

"Well, there is oil near Taiwan, in the waters near there." I have never even heard anyone say this. I am unsure from where Wang got this particular explanation, or whether oil-rich oceans adjacent to Taiwan is even true. Maybe he means that the Taiwan Strait would be a valuable commercial passageway, or that Taiwan would be strategically situated for China to increase influence in the Pacific. I am dumbfounded, but nonetheless I respond,

"No, no. That might be a reason why *China* may want Taiwan under China, but that is not a reason *for Taiwan* to want to annex into China. That'd be as if—"

The point is obvious to Chris and he beats me to it; he interrupts me, saying to Wang, "That's like we invaded Iraq and claimed it for our own purely because there are profitable oil fields there."

Wang immediately sees how off-kilter his answer is. He probably just had not had time to gather and order his thoughts, the discourse focusing on China's legitimacy in its claims being new in our conversation. I give him the benefit of the doubt, and post to him another opportunity to answer the question,

"So Wang, what are the reasons Taiwanese should want to be annexed into China?"

This time, Wang takes a more substantial moment to consider his answer. "Well, Taiwan can benefit from being with China."

I've heard this one too many times, from pro-China people of all stripes, Chinese, American, and even Taiwanese—and this answer still, absolutely, has never made sense to me.

"Yes, yes I know there are a lot of economic advantages of business partnerships with China," I say to Wang, "but plenty of countries have beneficial business partnerships with each other, without any need to unify as countries. It is only China's threatening and wanting to force Taiwan to eventually unify, coupling their threats with deceptive enticements: 'Your economy will join with ours and you can benefit!'

"But imagine the world without China's threat and China's forceful mandate for Taiwan to annex: both sides could obviously still do business with each other, Taiwan could benefit anyway, and so could China."

With another of Wang's reasons of why Taiwan should annex into China temporarily refuted, we're back again.

Cautious to refrain from becoming an aggressor myself, in my head I analyze my content of emotion, making sure a question does not become a condemnation, and I ask a third time, "So what reason does Taiwan, the Taiwanese, have that they should annex with China?"

Wang's eyes are fixed in the air as, in his mind, he scans through the information he knows, the truisms so often affirmed. His eyes suddenly lift up to mine. "Taiwan can come under China, and keep their system like Hong Kong and—"

"No!" I have interrupted Wang, I regret having done so, but the interruption's already occurred, so I go on, "But it is exactly like Hong Kong and Macao that Taiwan does *not* ever want to be."

I can see that in my confidence at this diametrically opposite view I just interjected, Wang already senses that his original view is faulty, even before I have given explanation.

I elaborate, "Hong Kong and Macao that you mention, these territories once separate from China now under China's system, have lost their rights continually since becoming under that system. Take for instance their rights and voting for their own local officials before Hong Kong's takeover: recently, more and more of their laws and public officials are being dictated from and by Beijing."[18] I wonder how much of this Wang, and even more so Chris,

---

18   Human Rights Watch has been one watchdog organization diligently tracking, vocalizing, and in so doing, fighting back the violations to democracy and human rights in Hong Kong since China's takeover in 1997.

In 2001, HRW published a "Letter from Scholars Based in Hong Kong," concerning the "prolonged detention of several scholars by the authorities in the last six months," and the "secrecy and non-transparent procedures adopted by the Mainland authorities in the detention of these scholars." (http://www.hrw.org/campaigns/china/scholars/mak_letter.htm)

In 2002, an HRW open letter, concerning the impending implementation of Article 23 to Hong Kong's constitution, warned that the law would "seriously undermine civil liberties and civil society in Hong Kong." The letter went on to explain,

"The proposed law's definition of 'seditious publications,' under which those who publish information inciting others to 'commit treason, secession or subversion' or 'endangering the stability of China and Hong Kong' can be jailed for seven years, is certain to have a chilling effect on the free flow of information. Much political commentary could be construed by some as inciting others to 'commit treason, secession or subversion.' If an individual wishes to express such sentiments it is his or her right. Acts, not words, should be punishable in a modern, rights-respecting society.

Use of the term 'stability' also raises serious concerns...It is a term that should not be introduced into Hong Kong law, as no editor or journalist will know when they have crossed

the line from legal into illegal speech, and no government can adequately assure publications that a future government will not misuse such a provision.

Human Rights Watch is particularly concerned that the proposed new laws under Article 23 give the Secretary for Security wide authority to ban local and foreign political organizations. According to the proposals, a declaration by the Chinese government that an organization endangers China's national security could be sufficient grounds for triggering investigations (or harassment) and possibly for a subsequent ban of a Hong Kong organization. This greatly increases the possibility of Chinese government intervention in Hong Kong. This provision introduces Chinese law and Chinese political control into Hong Kong through the back door, and is a clear violation of both the letter and spirit of the Basic Law.

This is particularly worrying since the statements of senior Chinese government officials make it appear that the impetus for the changes to Hong Kong's legal system has come not from the people of Hong Kong, but rather from Beijing...

Confidence in the independence of Hong Kong's legal system was further undermined by comments from senior officials, including the Secretary for Security, that the views of Beijing will be given weight when deciding whether to prosecute the Hong Kong media under Article 23 of the Basic Law.

In this context, of particular concern to Human Rights Watch is that the proposals for the implementation of Article 23 are similar to national security laws on the Mainland. As Human Rights Watch has documented over the past decade, in China similar subversion laws are regularly used to convict and imprison journalists, labor activists, Internet entrepreneurs, and academics. The Chinese government has tried and sentenced many activists who used the Internet to promote causes ranging from political change to worker rights. All were charged with subversion. Now that Hong Kong is part of China, these examples, taken together with the proposed language of the new subversion laws, give reason for concern that human rights in Hong Kong may be under threat." (http://www.hrw.org/press/2002/12/hongkong1223ltr.htm)

In a 2002 article in the *International Herald Tribune* entitled, "Hong Kong: Liberties in Doubt," the Director of HRW's Asia Division pointed to the "recent cave-in by Hong Kong to pressure from Beijing to enact laws against subversion, sedition, secession and theft of state secrets," and noted that "the muted response from key governments was surprising and disappointing." He gave one explanation: possibly the U.S. and other countries were "wary of stirring up a debate with Beijing over U.S. interference in the 'internal affairs' of Hong Kong, which is, after all, a part of China." (http://hrw.org/english/docs/2002/10/11/china12888.htm)

In 2004, HRW concluded,

"The Chinese government's new interpretation of the Basic Law pushes back the day when Hong Kong people will be able to exercise their right to choose their political leaders... The decision means that electoral reforms can only be initiated by Beijing's hand-picked Chief Executive, and bars Hong Kong's legislature from taking any action without his approval...

knows. How could anyone have not known about the hundreds of thousands of protesters who have taken to the streets of Hong

The new interpretation suggests that Beijing's goal is to preserve the status quo. At present, a majority of seats in Hong Kong's Legislative Council (LegCo) are elected by narrowly defined professional groups, while the Chief Executive is chosen by an election committee under the effective control of Beijing. Continuing with the current system would ignore the provisions in the Basic Law annexes that allow for amendments to Hong Kong's election system after 2007 and the obligation in Articles 45 and 68 of the Basic Law to move toward universal suffrage for the election of the Chief Executive and LegCo..."

In the article, the Executive Director of HRW Asia was quoted as saying, *"This looks like China and Tung have played a game of bait and switch with the Hong Kong people, suggesting an openness to more democratization just after the handover in 1997 but now making it clear that it is not in the offing. This interpretation contradicts both the spirit of the Basic Law and the expectations of Hong Kong people."* (http://hrw.org/english/docs/2004/04/07/china8409.htm)

Early this summer, on May 1st, 2008, the *Wall Street Journal Asia* published an editorial that followed the past months' international hot topic—pro-Tibet protests at nearly every global stop of the Olympic torch relay—to its stop in Hong Kong:

"...the Olympic torch has finally landed on "friendly" soil in Hong Kong. But the sporting symbol still hasn't escaped controversy. If anything, the uproar in the territory is about something broader than Tibet: The issue is free speech.

Over the past week, at least seven international activists have been deported trying to enter Hong Kong...

The Britons, Canadians and Danes turned away were planning peaceful protests related to such issues as China's human-rights record..."

The article cited another infringement upon Hong Kong's freedom of speech:

"Separately, the social networking Web site Facebook suspended the profiles of two local activists who either advocate for democracy in Hong Kong or protest on behalf of Tibet...

Raymond Wong, a local radio host, tells us he had 3,000 'friends' on his profile and used his Facebook site to publicize his writings and radio broadcasts. Christina Chan, a 21-year-old philosophy student, says she used her profile to organize a pro-Tibet protest. Ms. Chan had already been questioned by police about her protest plans before her account was suspended...

The timing of these cases has set tongues wagging about the limits of free speech in Hong Kong. The decisions at the border might not have been so controversial had they been made by a democratically elected and accountable government. Instead, the torch is casting light in its own way on Hong Kong's need for democratic reform." (http://online.wsj.com/article/SB120958333906057121.html)

Kong in the past years?[19] Hundreds of thousands of people who not long ago had their full democratic freedoms, who are slowly having those rights and freedoms stripped away, and who wanted to voice in unison, in protest, to Beijing and to the world that this is not their will.

I say again, "That is exactly what Taiwan does NOT want,"

—and here, I take a turn from my pathos, Taiwan's pathos, to my logos, Taiwan's logos, two forces of which together are the dismantler, the anti-missile, we have at our disposal to win this argument, for Taiwan to stay free—

"and even more, Hong Kong is not even a justifiable representative of what Taiwan could be. Hong Kong was only handed over and annexed to China because by contract, Hong Kong had always been agreed-upon to be returned from British rule to the

---

19   After the 1 million person marches in 1989 in response to the Tiananmen Square massacre, the next substantial protest that took place in Hong Kong came in 2003 when 500,000 people took to the streets on July 1, the anniversary of Hong Kong's handover to China. This large protest by Hong Kong's aggrieved citizens, directed at the proposed "Subversion Laws" in Article 23, led to the resignations of top administrators in the Hong Kong Special Administrative Region and the suspension of Article 23. (http://news.bbc.co.uk/2/hi/asia-pacific/3050056.stm) This 2003 protest has been the largest in Hong Kong since the handover and is commonly referred to as the showing of Hong Kong citizens' dissatisfaction with the retreat of democracy and individual rights, and the broken promise of "One Country, Two Systems" under Beijing.

On July 1, 2004, months after "Beijing ruled out universal suffrage and the election of a chief executive over the near term and at the same time called pro-democracy activists 'unpatriotic,'" 200,000 protesters marched in downtown Hong Kong. Beijing's political maneuvers "infuriated residents who have turned a public holiday meant to celebrate a return to Chinese hands into a day to vent their frustration at Beijing rule." (http://www.cnn.com/2004/WORLD/asiapcf/07/01/hk.anniversary/index.html)

Chinese after a set number of years. Absolutely nothing like that has ever been the case for Taiwan, and moreover, Taiwan and its people have experienced its own history for the past centuries and decades up to democracy and freedom, now, today."

At this last mention, I can tell Wang has in mind a rebuttal. But he does not interrupt me, he is more measured than I, he is less emotional—a Chinese patriotic nationalist, indeed, but not one to fire off belligerent confrontation, not one to try to intimidate me in any way, he is a thinker. I believe, I daydream in the span of a few seconds...

that in some fantastic world, if he, Wang, were the embodiment of the CCP, or whatever government it is that made decisions for China, despite Wang's seeming consistent belief that "Taiwan must be/become a part of China," this longstanding, grave, and tenuous impasse of the two countries across the Taiwan Strait would have that real chance for progress; Taiwan, China, and the world would truly have access to an eventual, peaceful, resolution of this complicated Taiwan issue, sooner rather than after it's too late. Wang's name, in Chinese, is the word for "king." What if Wang were king? (What a silly notion.) Or what if China's leadership had the capacity for real dialogue, for candid speaking and listening, for assessing and reconsidering their inherited truisms-sans-reasons? Is China's hermetic leadership capable of being influenced by external pressures, a change in the sea of outside processes? Doesn't any entity's leadership

evolve over time, don't the old calcified authoritarians eventually die one by one, as new people replace
them, whomever they may be? Isn't that the key component in how Taiwan eventually became a free democracy, and couldn't this same fact of political death
and life facilitate China's ability to change its aggression towards Taiwan?

I snap out of my daydream, as Wang has regrouped his
thoughts: in what he says, he is genuine, I see, his real beliefs, it
is evident, he (now, more than before) wears on his sleeve: his
approach to me is bare, truly inquisitive, I read on his face the
reaching-out to communicate, in his eyes resting on me simply
the acknowledgement of human being not dogmatic ideology, in
his posture natural facing me implying we might as well be taking
a stroll, two friends through a path in the woods with nothing on
our minds except the presence and exchange with the other, taking advantage of two minds and faces in real conversation, con-
necting, or actually attempting so (Wang is young like me, in fact,
just slightly younger than me; aren't those in the world at our
age, Wang and I, the generation who, in a dozen/two dozen or so
years, will be the subsequent faces, the minds, and the decisions
from where stances on all of these sides will have evolved and
replaced the present situation, by that time, in the near future?—
isn't this evolution of generations, and the potential for free will,
the slivers of possibility for thoughts free of indoctrination, alive,
the same story of adjustment-transformation that has repeated
itself generation after generation that allows for new states of being, of becoming?): Wang reminds me of my mention concerning

Taiwan's own historical progression to democracy and freedom. He asks me, somewhat rhetorically, reflecting-out-loud, "What is freedom, freedom as you say—what is it defined as. You say Taiwan has gotten their own 'democracy and freedom,' just like there is here. And everyone just believes it. But those are really just terms and everyone just believes it."

Without need for his further elaboration, he is already right in ways, because democracy and freedom are two words that are

(1) very loaded,

(2) very capricious (depending on the purpose of use, and who's speaking), and

(3) very vague,

and I use those two words as the central anchor, or more so, the absolute soul of my thoughts for Taiwan, my arguments against China. Just in this document, I have already built subsequent theses upon these vehicles, dozens of instances, without explaining or explicitly defining my vehicle. Democracy. Freedom. It's not that I don't have concrete definitions and characteristics in mind that hold meaning inside those terms,[20] those terms that drive me

---

20   In my own self-reflection over the years, I have concluded that the contours of my own unflinching value placed on the terms "democracy" and "freedom" comes from (1) my eventual understandings, in transition to my adulthood, of the contexts of memories I have as an elementary school-aged child in Taiwan, attending pro-democracy rallies, protesting against the authoritarian state, against the government's ruthless jailing and persecution of journalists, (2) my American birth and coming-of-age, loving the self-agency, prosperity, openness, possibilities free-of-persecution even when one might speak out critically against the government, and the tremendous benefits—or more appropriately, blessings—of America's "free and democratic" system of a society of the people, by the people, and for the people, etc., and (3) my learnings of societies that conversely failed to have those approaches, that were diametric to "free," counter to "democratic," and the dire tragedies of human beings within those situations, such as people

to speak up for Taiwan, to work towards those particular senses of universal rights and wrongs. Instead, the trip-up that Wang has pointed out here, I believe, is when in speaking of issues that spring from "democracy & freedom," we fail to constantly reiterate the very real contours of these virtues—and conversely, the explicit tragedies to humanity when "democracy & freedom" are lacking or absent—or, we forget the important task to re-educate the same in every new generation[21]. Even I, sometimes in such constant blabbing-on about preserving Taiwan's sovereignty, fail to elaborate in speech or in my own head, the foundational case for the democracy itself—so that over time, when asked, in an instance like this, by Wang, my speech feels like a tinge of windy rhetoric, and I feel empty for a slight moment. Only in taking another moment to remind, to pour into, to fill the jars that are these words, does one stay on point and keep the vigilant purpose, because, like any dynamic liquid, democracy and freedom, however hard-won, without a tight lid, whether subjected to pressure or sitting stagnant over time, can also lose meaning and evaporate.

I can see that Wang genuinely feels an affinity, as poignant and indescribable as to be something closest to a kind of love, for democracy and freedom. Otherwise, he would not have worked so hard, in his mind, in his choice of national surveillance as the topic of his journalism class paper, to define it with more and

---

I have read about and met who have survived through the worst instances in Communist China, Nazi Germany, anarchic Haiti, authoritarian Sudan, etc.

21   Here, a useful recent text is Naomi Wolf's 2007 pamphleteer-style book—coincidentally a similar style of book as this here—called *The End of America: Letter of Warning to a Young Patriot*. In the first paragraph of Chapter 1, she writes, "It is when memories are faint about coercive tactics that worked to control people in the past that people can be more easily controlled in the present."

more precision, gathering news, information, experiences, and thoughtful comparisons over the years of his young lifetime, despite his inability—or at least, in this afternoon's conversation with us thus far—to directly criticize China, his country, on these two counts. Maybe his love comes from the outsider (relative to China) experience of having lived his formative teenage years in democratic Japan, and of course being in America now. Or maybe love of democracy and political freedom is actually inherent, an idiosyncrasy of simply being born human, which we all are—and thus, a constant and innate component of humanity?

Wang is eager to expound on a topic that, both Chris and I could tell, he has enjoyed writing about so far in his paper: "If you're using the terms freedom and democracy that Taiwan has got, and you're comparing it with here... Are we really as free here?" Wang mentions the subtle deteriorations in the U.S., pointing out that cell phone companies have been forced to cooperate with the government, to invade the right to privacy of American citizens. He does not even need to go on to mention that arrests and detainments of American citizens without due process, and the ignominious un-American torture practices carried out by, and in the name of, America at Guantánamo Prison, because I have been let down by my country without Wang needing to say so, and I have already been cognizant of too many of these depressing acts by my shamed country since 9/11.

"Yeah," I mention, "the Patriot Act's really messed up a lot of things," is all I can muster up.

Wang continues, "You know, in a freedom ranking of the nations of the world—and keep in mind the U.S. always says they want to spread freedom all over the world—the U.S. is ranked only number 50."

I know. I know. Wang, this time I'm with you on this condemnation.

Through our conversation, this is a detour of a different sort; but, best that I can, I reengage my energies to the overall and initial purpose of our discussion: "I know that there are chips in every single democracy that calls itself free, there are many times, and various ways to look at the functioning and broken parts of a democracy—and that is definitely the case in America today, and in America at other troubled parts of its history (during Red Scare; pre-Civil Rights; during World War Two)..."

I gather my thoughts while I breathe, in, pause, because nailing down the whole point of all this is deceptively hard and essentially important.

I continue, "But what we're talking about here is the society, at its foundation, that Taiwan has reformed, transformed and evolved into." As much so as butterfly out of its cocoon or tree out from its seed—there may be deformities in the tree or mutations in the butterfly that constantly need further evolution for perfection of its virtue, but as a whole—neither is meant to ever morph back into its original shell.

"Taiwan and 23 million Taiwanese

"—by their constitutional, truly upheld, freedom of speech, freedom of press, freedom of religion, freedom from individual persecution by its governing body, guarantee of individual protection in the rule of law, and freedom to regularly vote for the local and national government officials who lead—

"have embraced the basis for a country that is free and democratic, and I think that *that* in itself is a universal cause to recognize Taiwan, and reason plentiful to protect Taiwan, propagate what Taiwan has achieved, and fight for its sovereignty, allowing the Taiwanese to go where they may go."

x. Where our conversation ends, and—in the answer of our silence—the single consensus, the precise next step that is inarguable and crucial for peaceful resolution on all sides

Where has Chris gone?

At some point, I guess, Wang and I had gotten so engaged in back and forth, up and down, inside and outside discussion that I believe neither of us had noticed Chris having left us to go on a brief lunch break.

I myself take a break from the table, I transport another few crates filled with envelopes sealed with books across the room, and when I come back, Chris is back.

"Hey Chris," says I.

"Hey Chris," says Wang.

"Hey guys," says Chris.

Pause. We silently begin, and continue to stuff envelopes.

After some meditation over everything, I come to the final, and really, the main point I want to say, the main point that I want to hear for a response from those in hearing range, those who are listening. And here goes:

"Okay, so this Taiwan and China thing. There's a lot of different viewpoints on where Taiwan came from, where Taiwan is now, what Taiwan should be.

"For instance, there's the Chinese view, the Taiwanese view, and even in Taiwan there're different background people with different views of what Taiwan came from and what Taiwan is.

"But there is one absolute question that no one from the Chinese view—not you, not any pro-China American politicians, not anyone who has ever been in the CCP—can give any type of logical moral answer to:

"That is: how in the world can China justify the deadly, constant aggression, the not only always on the verge, but continually growing arsenal of missiles at the ready, offensive military exercises, and assaulting or decapitation threats of force, all geared towards 23 million men, women, boys and girls of Taiwan, living in full democracy, with the most basic proven consensus that they want to keep their current freedoms, and be free to decide their own upcoming path in democracy?"...

...And within the profound silence in answer to that question—the seed at the core of all surrounding context, all conundrums and concerns on the paths moving forward, distilled singularly to how China, or anyone, can justify the deadly arsenal of non-negotiation aimed at Taiwan—is contained the dark-yet-hopeful key to stepping ahead on all remaining Taiwan-China issues. Or at least that's what I think.

February 15th, 2008 @ Housing Works Bookstore Café basement

Exterior street-view of Housing Works Bookstore Café

www.HumanityAtStake.com

Appendix A:

Author's March 2004 Online petition echoing Taiwan's historic 2-28 Hand-in-Hand Rally: "Supporting the People of Democratic Taiwan Against China's Missile Deployment"

Taiwan's Hand-in-Hand Rally on March 28th, 2004. Taichung County, Taiwan.

To: 23 million Citizens of Taiwan, Democracies of the World, Belligerent Govt. of China

For the 23 umillion citizens of democratic Taiwan, threats from China to their democracy and self-determination are constant, and growing. Today is a critical time to understand the story of Taiwan, and for you and I to voice support of the democracy that Taiwan has become.

On February 28, 2004, a heartfelt cry of pain, frustration, determination, and unity came from one of the leading democracies in East Asia. An estimated 1.5 million citizens of Taiwan lined the western border of Taiwan, from the northern to the southern tip of the island, and joined and raised their hands collectively to form a 500-km human chain. Many in tears, they shouted the slogans, "love peace, oppose missiles," "unity among ethnic groups," and "join hands to protect Taiwan."

February 28th marks what was once a scathing scar for the people of Taiwan, now designated National Peace Day. That day in 1947 was the beginning of a nightmarish year, when tens of thousands of Taiwanese were systematically murdered by the Kuomingtang (KMT) Nationalists recently arrived from China. When the Japanese colonizers of Taiwan surrendered to the Allies in 1945, the Allies allowed Chiang Kai-shek and his KMT regime temporary administrative control of Taiwan. Unfortunately for the people of Taiwan, the KMT's dictatorial rule soon became brutal (and permanent, as later Mao Tze-tung and the Communist Revolution in China forced the KMT regime to flee and set up headquarters in Taiwan). Within a few years, the KMT wiped out a generation of Taiwan's intellectual middle class and cast a thick cloud of hardship and terror upon the island's people. During the next 40 years, as Taiwan endured the brutality and suppression of KMT martial law rule, mention of the traumatic "2-28 Massacre" was forbidden, and human rights was a faraway dream in the midst of continual murders, imprisonments, government blacklists, and what many historians have called the "iron fist" rule of the KMT military regime over the island's people.

However, in the past twenty years, through the sacrifices and passion of multitudinous Taiwanese and foreign democracy advocates, Taiwan has liberalized tremendously both socially and politically. Nearly a decade after the lifting of martial law, in 1996, Taiwan held its first-ever democratic election, and in 2000, the country peacefully transferred power to the elected opposition party, ending 50 years of KMT rule. Taiwan has miraculously evolved into a full democracy and a leader and champion of human rights in the world. U.S. lawmakers have repeatedly termed Taiwan a "model for democracy" in Asia.

While within Taiwan, such incredible strides have been made in so short a time, outside of Taiwan, China's strong-arm forces still act to threaten, intimidate, and subvert the 23 million Taiwanese's ability to freely exercise their democracy. China considers Taiwan a "renegade province" and has accepted no other basis for negotiation except that Taiwan consent to annexation—and China has repeatedly demonstrated the use of military force as a means to that end.

China is currently pointing 496 missiles at Taiwan from only 100 miles away. In the weeks and days before Taiwan's elections in '96 and '00, China fired "missile tests" off the shore of Taiwan; and in the upcoming Taiwanese elections in March, China is projected to again mobilize military forces in an attempt to intimidate the 23 million citizens of Taiwan. Many international military analysts and strategists even worry that China's accelerated buildup, in the past and upcoming years, could soon give it the edge and capability to forcefully overtake Taiwan.

Whatever the question on Taiwan's national agenda may be—whether it is, "Does Taiwan want to declare de jure independence, putting into words on the world's stage its already obvious de facto independence?" "Should Taiwan ever accept an eventual 'One China, Two Systems,' policy similar to that of Hong Kong?" "Why is Taiwan still not allowed participation in the United Nations or the World Health Organization, even as the SARS outbreak hit at home last year?" or even the most basic democratic question, "Whom should I vote for?"—China's missiles, military buildups, and aggressive threats unfortunately play the same role that a bully plays, when a class and its individuals attempt to formulate opinions and decisions. How could one not feel nervous, walking into a voting booth with an armed aggressor pointing weapons at you, constantly threatening to shoot at every movement?

On February 28, 2004, the people of Taiwan once again far exceeded the expectations of doubters—just like they surprised China by going to the voting booths in both '96 and '00 despite China's firing missiles into the Taiwan Strait. On stage with representatives from all of Taiwan's Hakka, Hokhlo, mainlander, aborigine, and other various ethnic groups, President Chen announced to the 500-km-long chains of Taiwanese, "The Taiwan people have used the most simple, solemn and sacred method of hands linked in hand to express to the world their resolve to protect Taiwan's sovereignty and democratic development, economic prosperity and lasting peace in the Taiwan Strait." Asked why they joined the rally, a participant in Taipei responded, "We joined the rally to tell China that Taiwanese people hold the ultimate say in their own future." Another woman, who brought five of her children and grandchildren to join the chain, responded that she was angry at the Chinese missile deployment, asking, "How can we remain silent?"

On February 28, 2004, Taiwan's President Chen called the historic 1.5-million-person human chain a "great wall of democracy," and added, "We showed the world our determination to recognize Taiwan and protect Taiwan." Let us now all show that we have heard the voice of the people of Taiwan, and that we echo and support their rights to democracy, self-determination, and freedom from military intimidations. For peace, for human rights of the people of Taiwan, for security in East Asia, China must immediately withdraw its missiles aimed at Taiwan.

Sincerely,

_____

To see the worldwide signatures and responses to this 2004 petition online, or to find links to additional current petitions, advocacy actions and activities, please refer to www.HumanityAtStake.com.

Appendix B:
May 13, 2008: Letter received by the author of *Humanity At Stake* from Member of Congress Ileana Ros-Lehtinen

Taiwan faces a historic hour as a new President prepares to assume office in Taipei. The delicate diplomatic balance in the Taiwan Strait, which has lasted for more than a generation, has as its corner stone the Taiwan Relations Act passed by the Congress over a quarter century ago.

The Taiwanese-American community has been at the forefront in maintaining those cherished, traditional ties between our two peoples which assures the security of Taiwan. The torch is now passing to a new generation of Taiwanese-Americans who will be called upon to make the same diligent efforts as those who have gone before to maintain strong ties between the U.S. and Taiwan.

Beijing feels great discomfort that just across a narrow strait lies this island of Taiwan, a thriving democracy. Its continued existence belies the claim that Chinese culture is incompatible with democratic ideals, that the extremely talented Chinese people must be forever subservient to the will of the dictatorial Mandarins who supposedly know what is best for them. This condescending attitude dismisses the creative vitality of a people who have sustained for millennia one of the world's greatest cultures. And the people of Taiwan and their dynamic democracy prove the falsehood of these claims.

The Chinese regime's leadership's continued desire to isolate Taiwan stems partially from the discomfort felt because of Taiwan's continuing democratic success. And the threat to peace in the Taiwan Strait, therefore, remains all too real.

The Taiwan Relations Act calls upon the U.S. Government to make available those defensive weapons that Taiwan needs to ensure its security. I was especially pleased, therefore, that the House adopted the resolution I introduced in September 2007 "declaring that it shall continue to be the policy of the United States, consistent with the Taiwan Relations Act, to make available to Taiwan such defense articles and services as may be necessary for Taiwan to maintain a sufficient self-defense capability."

I have been, and will continue to be, one of Taiwan's best friends in Congress. And I will seek to ensure that Taiwan will continue as a beacon of democracy shining its light directly across the strait in the very heart of Tiananmen Square.

Ileana Ros-Lehtinen
Member of Congress

(May 13th, 2008)

To see whether your Representative and Senators are members of the Congressional or Senate Taiwan Caucuses, respectively, links and actions are available for perusal at www.HumanityAtStake.com

Postscript:

Why? The reason, in few words and 1,000 explosive pictures across the page

This is a picture of Taiwan,
to the east of China's eastern border.

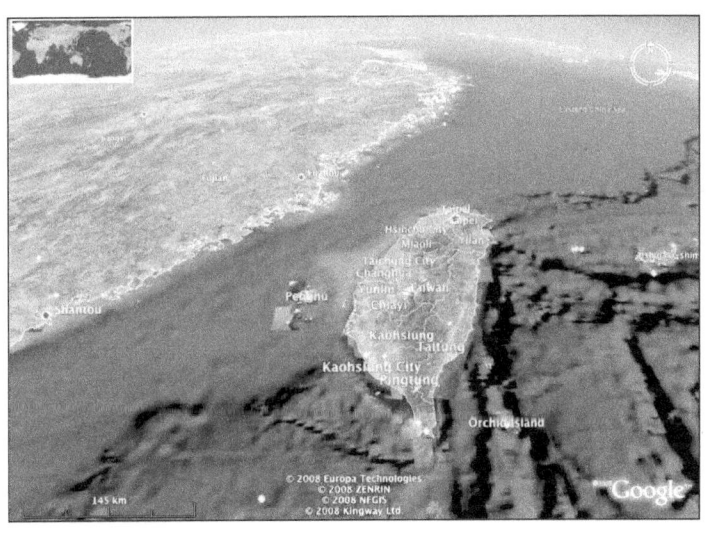

Image courtesy of Google Earth™ mapping service;
Europa-Technologies; ZENRIN; NFG1S; Kingway Ltd.

This is a picture of China, to the west of Taiwan's western border.

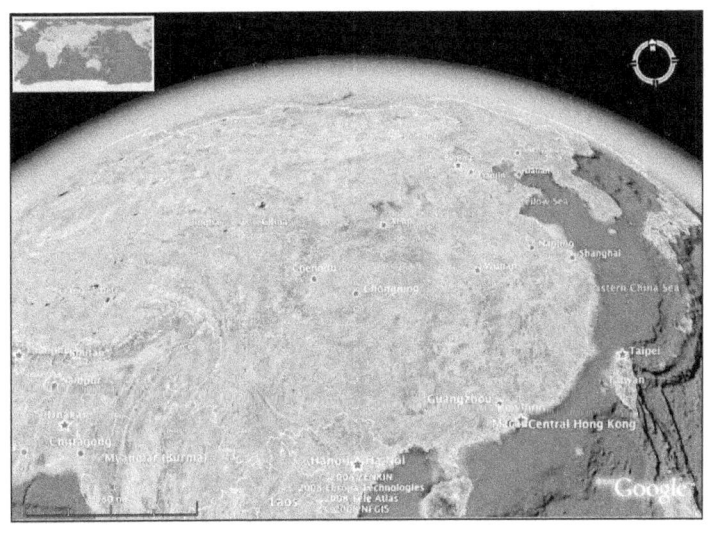

Image courtesy of Google Earth™ mapping service;
ZENRIN; Europa-Technologies; Tele Atlas: NFG1S

This is a picture of 1 real Chinese/People's Liberation Army ballistic missile.

Photo in public domain / Department of Defense / Wikimedia Commons

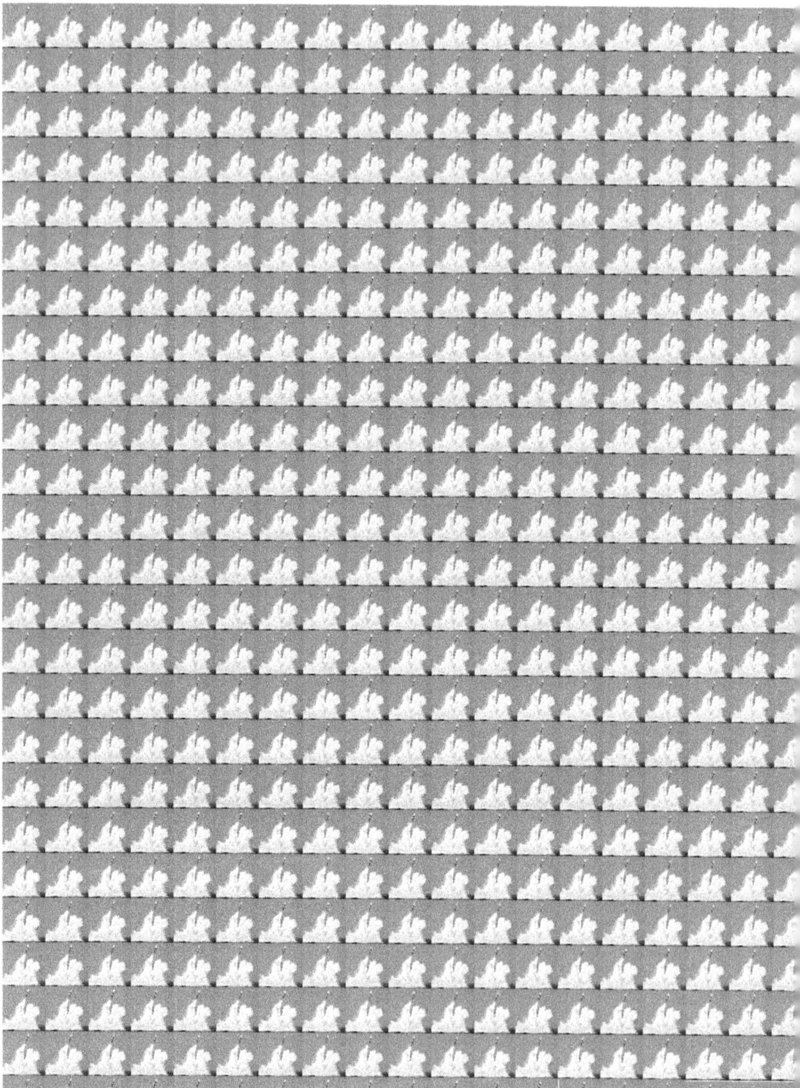

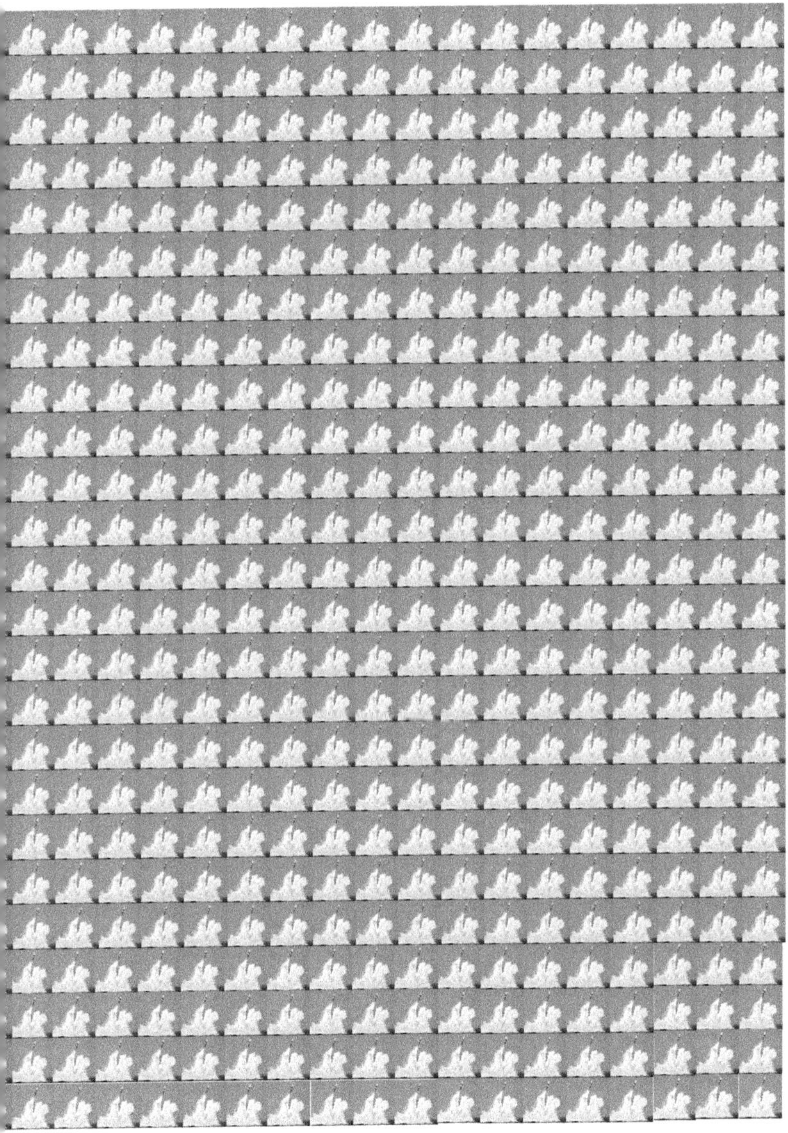

... That was 1,000 pictures of real Chinese/People's Liberation Army ballistic missiles

In 1998, there were **150** Chinese/People's Liberation Army ballistic missiles aimed at Taiwan.

4 years after, in 2002, there were **300** Chinese/People's Liberation Army ballistic missiles aimed at Taiwan.

3 years after, in 2005, there were **730** Chinese/People's Liberation Army ballistic missiles aimed at Taiwan.

2 years after, in 2007, there were **900** Chinese/People's Liberation Army ballistic missiles aimed at Taiwan.

1 year later, now in 2008, there are **1,400** Chinese/People's Liberation Army ballistic missiles aimed at Taiwan.

For Taiwanese, the reasons for disarming China's military and political aggression are more than obvious.

For Chinese, the reasons for disarming China's military and political aggression are—from the Chinese government, so far—unheard of, given the drumming up of Chinese nationalism, militarism, and the dogmatic view of some "destiny of reunification for all of Greater China's historical territories," in the past decades. But a sober and more logical look at this viewpoint can only be helpful to the humanity, health, and prosperity of the Chinese people, not to mention that disarmament is the only assured way towards avoiding the tragedies of military conflict.

For Americans, then, if not only for the preservation of the 23 million Taiwanese people living in free democratic society, Americans should also want the disarming of China's military and political aggression towards Taiwan...

- because historically, America provided the role model and support for Taiwan's ability to become the democracy that it is today, and it is in America's interest to disarm the growing intimidator (PRC) that will threaten the sustainability of Taiwan's currently successful democracy.

- because America has had a healthful economic relationship with Taiwan—a country with amongst the highest economic, social and political compatibility with America, and a country which has been amongst the top trading partners with America for the past decades—and both countries would economically prosper with the decreased threat on Taiwan from China.

- because at the rate that China's military and missile arsenal directly aimed at Taiwan is growing, China is exponentially gaining the potential to deliver what China terms a "sudden fatal blow" to Taiwan—in essence, with a sudden deployment of overwhelming military offense, make obsolete Taiwan's limited abilities to defend itself (much less negotiate), and simultaneously "decapitate" Taiwan's political leadership to gain control of the country before allies like the U.S. have any chance to intervene. And if China suddenly, forcibly gained control of Taiwan, America would

  - become geopolitically threatened by the encroachment of China's domain further into the Pacific.

  - lose a crucial democratic strategic ally in East Asia

  - lose one of the most important real & symbolic embodiments of a successful transition to full democracy in the Eastern Hemisphere, and the most important embodiment of democracy in Asia.

Post-postscript:
What's At Stake

Ching Shui, Taiwan.

Taipei, Taiwan. 2008.

Taipei, Taiwan. 2006.

"Save your own future, oppose the One China market!" 2008.

"We are Taiwanese indeed." Taipei, Taiwan. 2008.

Taipei, Taiwan. 2008.

Flickr.com/CreativeCommons/, Attribution license: "TingChang"

What's At Stake | 103

New York City, USA. 2003.

Permission granted for photo. Katherine Chiu

"Oppose authoritarians. Return justice."
Taipei, Taiwan. 2008.

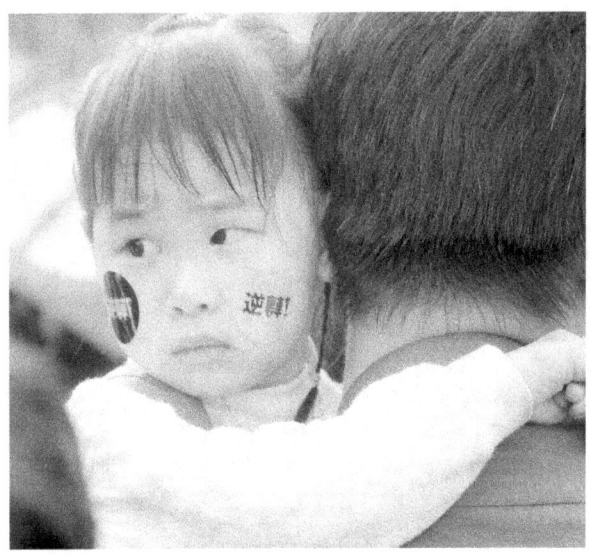

"Reverse the tide!" Taipei, Taiwan. 2008.

Taipei, Taiwan. 2008.

Tainan, Taiwan. 2008.

Tainan, Taiwan. 2008.

Taroco Gorge, Taiwan. 2007.

Taiwan. 2007.

Taroco Gorge, Taiwan. 2007.

Man who is a member of
Taiwanese aboriginal tribe.
2007.

Father & daughter presenting fish from river in Danye, Nantou, Taiwan. Author's cousin & uncle. 2003.

Photo by Abraham Young

Cold Spring of SuAu, in Ilan, Taiwan. Author with cousins. 2003.

Taiwan. 2006.

Tansui, Taiwan. 2001.

Class photo taken in Dahu-Miaoli, Taiwan. Author's father (back row, 5th from left). 1961.

Permission granted for photo. Ming-Lon Young

Taipei, Taiwan. Author's mother and uncle. 1962.

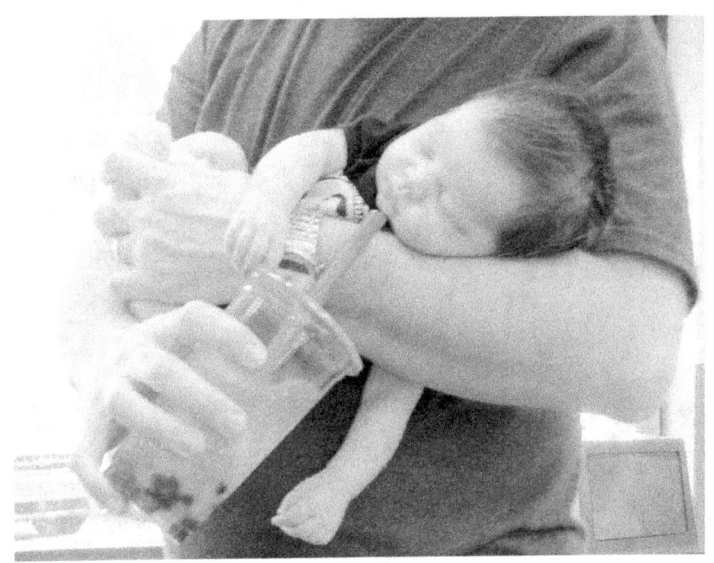

A baby is oblivious to the bubble tea. 2007.

Shihlin night-market in Taipei, Taiwan. 2006.

Over 400 Falun Dafa practitioners and their families. Banner: "Wishing Master Li a Happy Lunar New Year". Pingtung County, Taiwan. 2007.

Temple in Da-Chia, Central Taiwan. 2004.

Banner: "24 hours of sending our love to Tibet." Rally at National Taiwan Democracy Memorial Hall in Taipei. 2008.

Taiwan. 2007.

If you have a personal connection in/of Taiwan, and would like to add your own photo, text, etc. in this growing collection, please email HumanityAtStake@gmail.com with subject line "What's At Stake".

Readers' submissions will be added on each week at www.HumanityAtStake.com.

The Humanity At Stake Project
www.HumanityAtStake.com

Please continue your perusal, to see the worldwide participation of other readers, at the website. And leave your own mark and contribute your own thoughts in the interactive pages.

The www.HumanityAtStake.com website will be continually expanded, and as of this writing includes the following pages:

"√ Direct, quick-links to the full, original web pages of all references used throughout the footnotes of *Humanity At Stake*"
Browse/explore the full original sources as they appeared online and in print, exactly as the world saw them during the days of the event.

"√ What's At Stake: A Global Conversation Through Multimedia"
View other readers' contributions and/or add your own, to the extended Post-postscript, "What's At Stake".

"√ Start Your Advocacy Now!"
View the author's 2004 petition "Supporting the People of Democratic Taiwan Against China's Missile Deployment", as it appeared online; and see the 900+ worldwide signatures & impassioned comments. Also, many more avenues of involvement and advocacy are listed here.

"√ Tracking the # of PLA Missiles Aimed at Taiwan"

"√ Documenting the Un-'status-quo' Across the Taiwan Strait"

"√ Humanity At Stake: Interactive Forum"
Free-form interaction with other readers, supporters (or opponents), and strangers of *Humanity At Stake*

"√ Coalition of organizations/global citizens: 'To stand against China's missiles, and to stand with Taiwan's democracy & self-determination'"
View the growing list of worldwide organizations and individuals who have joined this Humanity At Stake coalition—or sign on your organization and yourself.